THE CLASH
AND ATTRACTION OF TWO CULTURES

THE CLASH
AND ATTRACTION

The Hispanic and Anglo-Saxon

Foreword by Jacques Barzun

LOUISIANA STATE UNIVERSITY PRESS

OF TWO CULTURES

Worlds in America

Angel del Río

Translated and Edited by
JAMES F. SHEARER

BATON ROUGE, 1965

FOREWORD

FEW enterprises are more liable to futility than those purporting to foster intellectual cooperation. The phrase covers, all too often, the clichés of tourism and the banalities of the visiting dignitary. That is why it is so refreshing, indeed invigorating, to pick up Angel del Río's small but compact work and find in it the solid substance of the historian, the shrewd estimates of the critic, and the voice of a man.

No one who has lived for any length of time in Europe or in North or South America will suppose that it is easy to speak of the continent where he resides. "Continent" when thus used is something that only a geographer can feel thoroughly able to define and describe. Anybody else is beset with diffidence and doubt, and the more intelligent he is, and the more traveled, the less he is sanguine about his chances of making a true general statement. "The Latin Americans have always been—thus and so." "In North America, the people believe—this or that." It is really quite impossible: the predicates would impose only on children in the cradle, to whom place names are but pegs for hanging dreams.

And since the readers in each of the contrasted cultures do know parts of their history and environment with a fierce

v

grasp of detail and meaning—the accepted meaning, often, which is very likely wrong—the writer who professes to bring a new understanding finds himself surrounded by traps and dilemmas and critics ready to pounce.

There is only one way out of the predicament: to be a scholar and make firm assertions backed by documents. This course of action leaves but one difficulty, which is how to keep from boring the reader. In short, the writing of a book addressed to two great peoples in the hope of showing each its own face so convincingly that it will trust the new presentment offered of the other amounts to a dare, a wager. Angel del Río has run the risk and won the reward. His book is meaty and yet light. He quotes many people but one steadily hears his voice. He plucks out of the void the telling instance, the relevant allusion, the proper name that vivifies an abstraction.

Yet as I remember him from the days of his young manhood, there was nothing of the daredevil or gambler about him. He was a mild man, contemplative, rather silent except when an idea possessed him. Then he was eloquent and his eye shone with the passion of the mind. He wore his cultivation and wide reading lightly; and like most academic men he never gave the impression that ideas, the past, or the lives of the great were academic. They were present to his consciousness, just as they are to us in his terse prose.

If every few years someone of comparable powers could produce a book, portable and readable like this one, about foreign cultures, singly or in contrast, there would be less need of expensive public relations programs abroad, one would hear fewer tiresome clichés about every country, and even banquet oratory might begin to carry a little ballast of thought. But for such books to be written, the author must have lived long, read much, and thought deep, and this is not given to all by merely wishing. Whoever turns the pages of this book will appreciate the truth of this observation by coming face to face with uncommon talent perfectly adapted to its purpose.

JACQUES BARZUN

Columbia University
March 1, 1965

CONTENTS

ix

INTRODUCTION

PUBLISHED here, in slightly amplified form, are English versions of the texts of two lectures delivered in various countries of South America under the auspices of the Congress for Cultural Freedom during the months of June, July, and August of 1959. We believe that the subject, with which the author has been continually concerned during his thirty years of interpreting Spanish culture in the United States, will not be devoid of interest to all those who would aspire to understand thoroughly what is occurring today in the two worlds we are comparing in these pages. The historical, cultural, and political implications are at once many and varied.

We have preserved, with only minor modification, the lecture style dictated by our original purpose, and it will be obvious that there has been no attempt to engage either in original investigation or to produce a work of historical or critical erudition. The pertinent bibliography, although scattered and incomplete, is immense. In the book by Stanley T. Williams —particularly in its references to Spain—or in other cited works, the reader will find indications useful in amplifying his information on general or specific aspects of the question. It is only with the idea of facilitating such a task that we have added a number of notes to a work which by its nature, that of essay-lecture, would not normally demand them.

The section dealing with the opinions certain Spanish writers and travelers have had of the United States is in the main new, a theme which, to the best of our knowledge, has not so far been treated by anyone.

In short, we believe that whatever value these two studies may have will be found especially in their synthesis of the subject and in their approach. We have aimed above all at objectivity. This we are convinced can be attained only by one who, like the author, is fully and equally identified with the two cultures and the two worlds here being scrutinized; with the Hispanic, since it is his by origin and its study his profession; with the American, since it is his by adoption, and by virtue of more than thirty years of professional activity in the field of university teaching in the United States.

Doubtless many will be surprised by the rather optimistic tone of our conclusions to the second lecture. Fortunately, there seems to have been a change of attitude on the part of the United States in turning greater attention toward the Hispanic-American problems to which we allude therein. In contrast to this, anti-Americanism or anti-Yankeeism, whether justified or not, has been on the increase in certain countries during recent months, and in some has manifested itself in virulent form. Everything indicates that relations between these two worlds are, at this very moment, passing through a difficult stage. This fact notwithstanding, we are convinced that our conclusions should not be modified to any substantial degree, in view of the historical perspective from which we approach our subject. Today we live avidly awaiting the latest news story, believing that the solution of complex problems, if not the very destiny of mankind, depends upon it. One too often forgets that historical processes are marked by a very slow period of gestation and that even in these tumultuous times it is only in minor ways, and after protracted vicissitudes, that peoples and cultures can deviate appreciably from a trajectory in which the past and their own characters have been the basic determinants. Keeping this fact firmly in mind, we have endeavored to study and understand the clash and attraction of the two great cultures of the New World. Perhaps we should add that although only infrequent reference is made to Brazil (in view of its autonomy and peculiar position within the Hispanic or Iberian bloc), implicitly it is included therein, although we are fully cognizant of the basic differences in its historical development as compared with other countries of similar culture.

ANGEL DEL RÍO

Columbia University
December 1, 1959

THE CLASH
AND ATTRACTION OF TWO CULTURES

PART I

SPAIN
AND THE UNITED STATES
A Historico-Cultural Survey

TWO intimately related facts should be emphasized as we approach the question of relations between the Hispanic and the Anglo-Saxon worlds in America: geographic propinquity and, in the area of Spain's historical past, the long period—almost a century and a half—of political, diplomatic, and cultural clash with the powerful republic of the north that was to deteriorate finally into armed conflict. When, with its newly won independence, the United States assumed a historical role among nations, it found Spain at its frontiers and in possession of the greater part of the continent she had discovered, colonized, and organized before any other European power.

Under such circumstances the inhabitants of the thirteen original colonies, Protestants and Puritans of English or Dutch extraction, felt themselves the inheritors of an old politico-religious rivalry, springing from the very beginning of the modern period. Before long they would justify their incipient expansionist spirit with the traditional hostility toward a people who, for more than two centuries, had been considered the champions of Counter-Reformist Catholicism and who, in consequence, were considered the principal enemy of their faith. Spain for the Puritan was the

5

incarnation of all the evils of the Black Legend* and of certain values—if indeed these were recognized—diametrically opposed to his own.

These two circumstances—proximity and clash of cultures —will determine, through a complex historical process, a series of antagonisms and attractions still operative in the relations between the two cultures, although there is not always a full awareness of this fact.

Thus the initial or immediate reaction of the average American to something Spanish or Hispanic is, in a majority of cases, one of scorn and bewilderment, be this in the intellectual, social, or moral domain. In other cases the reaction springs from an abysmal ignorance, by no means limited in every instance to the ordinary or uneducated individual. For example, the downgrading of Hispanic values in the academic and intellectual world is a most curious thing. This is probably an unconscious and involuntary devaluation, but it is no less obvious on that account. We professors of Spanish departments know how little we count, with rare exceptions, in the university councils or in the general teaching of the humanities. Such is the case, notwithstanding the noble tradition of Hispanic scholarship as well as the extent and general excellence of Spanish instruction in the United States. On the other hand, as we shall have occasion to see, this situation stands in sharp contrast to the accurate appreciation of certain Hispanic values on the part of a large number of writers.

It is a well-known fact that, with the exception of Cervantes, a Spanish name appears only rarely on those imposing lists to which certain avowed scholars ingeniously attempt to reduce the literary legacy of the world. There are histories of the European theatre where scarcely any men-

---

* The defamatory, and substantially false, interpretation of Spanish history. (Translator's note.)

tion is made of the *comedia* of Spain's Golden Age, so influential on the French and English drama. Knowledge of Spanish literature, save on the part of specialists, is ordinarily limited to the names of Cervantes, Lorca, and perhaps Ortega y Gasset. When Juan Ramón Jiménez received the Nobel Prize in 1956, few, even among the cultured, knew the name of the great poet, although he had long been a resident of the United States.

Lorca has been the one notable exception in recent times. However, when his plays are presented, decorations, costumes, and gestures make us think of a remote and exotic land, with a Mexican sarape or a hat thrown in gratuitously to lend an aura of local color. Actors, directors, and critics, although conscious in their way of the poetic and dramatic value of his theatre, only rarely succeed in penetrating what really constitutes the intrinsic nature of his art: the intimate fusion of poetry and reality, the essence of all Spanish art.

Casals, Segovia, Victoria de los Angeles, Picasso (generally considered a French painter), Miró, and Dalí, or Zuloaga, Sorolla, Granados, and Falla, of the preceding generation, are well-known names among lovers of the arts. All of which still does not prevent the average American from believing that bullfighters and flamenco dancers are the most genuine, and almost exclusive, Spanish artistic manifestations.

Because of its revealing nature, I should like to recall an event in which I played a part not long ago. The Dessoff Choir, a choral group of high artistic calibre, organized, during the month of January, 1959, a concert of Spanish Renaissance music, devoted exclusively to the work of Tomás Luis de Victoria. Two or three months prior to the performance I was asked to prepare a few historical notes on Victoria and his times for inclusion in the program. Other obligations prevented my doing so, although a friend had warned me of what would happen were I not to accept the assignment. Indeed, the day of the concert arrived, and the anonymous notes finally appearing in the program were limited, except for some extremely rudimentary data on the life of the composer, to certain innocuous allusions to Cervantes, Lope, El Greco, and Philip II (not overlooking the fury of the Inquisition). Moreover, the organizers of the function could find no more adequate a text for giving an idea of the Spain of the sixteenth century than the data on Barcelona collected by an obscure medical student, Thomas Plater, in 1599. In this account it was stated, among other things equally enlightening for an understanding of the art and spirituality of Victoria, that the Spanish people were given to all sorts of superstitions, that they were back-stabbers, that they were less cordial to foreigners than the French, etc. Finally, several paragraphs were devoted to the office of the Inquisition, to the cruelties committed here, and to the reigning animosity toward Lutherans.

The concert was excellent, but the matter has an added significance. These people were of a high cultural level and capable of interpreting the music of Victoria with great skill. Moreover, they were undoubtedly conscientious, as seen in the fact that they had contacted a person they deemed competent to prepare the notes. However, when they did not get the cooperation they sought, and had to rely on their own knowledge, they did not have the faintest suspicion of how utterly inadequate, false, and offensive their vision of Spain was—and this in a program that aspired to make known one of that country's great creators.

Of course, at times our collaboration and advice are given but go unheeded because they conflict with very deep-rooted, prevailing ideas. Something of the sort occurs with certain presentations of Lorca's theatre, or with reviews appearing in literary magazines of the few Spanish works that have been translated. In these instances ordinarily the incompetent judgment is preferred if it is more in accord with the general ideas of the public.

Let us recall, finally, that a number of years ago a gathering of poets of various nationalities was organized, and it occurred to no one in charge of the undertaking to invite Juan Ramón Jiménez, Jorge Guillén, or Pedro Salinas, Spanish poets who had already lived several years in the United States.

Concerning the inveterate nature of the most negative historical prejudices, let us turn to the testimony of Herbert Bolton (one of the most distinguished historians of Hispanic culture), who recalls some of the unquestioned midwestern beliefs in which he was reared as a youth.[1] Among these he points to the distrust with which Catholics, Mormons, and Jews were viewed; to the sense of superiority of the English and how their successors, the Americans, were God's chosen people; how all the history of America had developed between the forty-ninth parallel and the Rio Grande; and how the Americans had effectively ejected the Mexicans from New Mexico, Texas, Arizona, and California in order to build a great empire. Bolton adds that all these ideas were false, in whole or in part, but that it had cost him half a lifetime to discover that fact.

At the outset it is important to emphasize certain typical factors of a negative sort and to try later on for a more thorough understanding of a number of very complex relationships. These, I believe, are most revealing in their great contradictions, and show how, historically, two cultures in large measure diametrically different, repel and attract each other. It is the nature of our problem to have many facets, some of which would seem to contradict everything we have already said. For the moment, and still within the area of generalizations, one could point to a strange affinity between certain traits of the Spanish and American characters that transcends intellectual and historical prejudices.

If such an affinity is valid, I would say it is based on a similar concept of life and human personality. Spaniards and Americans seem to share an almost instinctive feeling—vital and not rational—about what we could call the whole man; the firm conviction that what really counts is the person, the individual. We are dealing with an evident feeling in the anarchical Spaniard and with a feeling deeply buried, but no less real, in the American—a being obviously sociable and even gregarious in nature.

There probably exists also the more or less conscious impression of the complementary character of both cultures: the Hispanic and the Anglo-American. This would explain the fact that, as we shall see, despite the ignorance of the average American about Spain, and notwithstanding grave historical conflicts, interest in Spanish culture has never disappeared in certain intellectual strata, an interest which in many instances has exceeded that aroused by other European cultures.

As for the ordinary American, it is paradoxical that, in spite of his prejudices, when for some reason he comes into direct, personal contact with Spanish life, he usually reacts with great enthusiasm and cordiality. In Spain I have had occasion to observe more than one typical Yankee trying to be more typically Spanish than the Spaniards themselves. This should not be considered in any way a novel reaction, especially if one recalls that certain Englishmen have traditionally reacted to Spanish life in a similar fashion.

I

B UT let us now summarize as succinctly as possible the historical conflict, the immediate antecedents of which stem from the year 1763 when, after the Seven Years' War, Spain gained possession of Louisiana. It was a conflict which was not to end until the War of 1898 over Cuba. It is to be noted in passing that the Spanish-American War has been the only national war of the United States. By this I mean between it and another nation prior to the international conflicts of the twentieth century. We are not considering the struggles with England, which were a prolongation of the War of Independence, or the war with Mexico, which was a part of the expansionist program of the United States in the Hispanic world.

The areas of dispute were many. But one must seek the roots of the friction in the historical coincidence that placed a young nation, astir from the outset with well-defined plans for expansion, opposite an old country weakened by a secular struggle against the forces of modern Europe and already well on the way toward the inevitable liquidation of its boundless empire.

It is a frequently forgotten fact that during the American Revolution, Spain, an ally of France and a rival of England, aided the rebellious colonies. But despite the efforts of Benjamin Franklin, Arthur Lee, and John Jay, envoys to Paris and Madrid, Spain never signed a treaty of alliance nor moved, save after the passage of considerable time, to grant official recognition to the new nation.

Although Spain's attitude was anti-British, she had to move with caution, conscious as she was of possible future dangers: for example, concern over the uncertain definition of her territorial limits and fears over the reaction of her own colonies, not long in emulating the example of those of England.

Pressure against her frontiers was not long in developing. "A decade before that event [the Louisiana Purchase] there were hundreds of American pioneers in the Spanish territory beyond the Mississippi; near the close of the eighteenth century the bishop of Louisiana reported that 'the Americans had scattered themselves over the country almost as far as Texas and corrupted the Indians and Creoles by the example of their own restless and ambitious temper.' Already promoters in the West had their eyes fixed on Mexico and were blowing up colorful dreams of imperial annexations to be realized in that direction." [2] Therefore the Americans were determined that the Mississippi River remain open to commercial traffic; Spain attempted merely to stem the tide. Slow negotiations were initiated, but Napoleon forced the Spanish government to return Louisiana to France and almost immediately sold it to Jefferson.

Spain protested in vain. Napoleon had not complied with the conditions stipulated in the Treaty of San Ildefonso, whereby France was to acquire possession of the returned territories, and in consequence he had sold something not legally his. Under renewed pressures the Spanish government was forced to yield. Before long it was confronted with another problem because Napoleon had purposely left the borders of Louisiana loosely defined. It seems that when the envoys James Monroe and R. R. Livingston importuned him to establish them more exactly, he replied cynically, "If obscurity did not already exist, perhaps it would be good policy to create it."

This deliberate lack of precision made it possible for the United States to reclaim Western Florida. Thus began a long chapter of diplomatic tensions that ended with the Florida sale treaty of 1819. If space permitted it would be interesting to examine the maze of intrigues, claims, charges, counter-charges, incidents, and threats arising during a more than fifteen-year period until an agreement was reached in these sundry matters. Besides the question of the acquisition of the two Floridas, with the interminable discussions over boundaries, negotiations were endlessly embroiled by the attacks of pirates and freebooters, by numerous incursions into the territories of Florida and Texas, by the occupation of Amelia Island, and, last but not least in gravity, by the actions of Mexican and South American agents, whose countries were already engaged in their wars of independence.

After clever debates and much haggling between John Quincy Adams, Secretary of State, and the Spanish minister, Luis de Onís, the treaty of 1819 was signed. The United States, at the same time that it rounded out its territory in the Southeast, gained unlimited access to the West and was now free to lend overt aid to the cause of Hispanic-American independence. For Spain this spelled the end of her dominion in what today is the territory of the United States; she extricated herself from an untenable situation and in so doing saved face, which seemed the only thing that mattered to the court of Madrid in this sad period of the country's decadence and the decline of its empire.

Let us now see how one of the most respected American

historians, Henry Adams, a descendant, moreover, of the Secretary of State who signed the treaty, sums up the question:

Hatred of a Spaniard was to the Tennesseean as natural as hatred of an Indian, and contempt for the rights of the Spanish government was no more singular than for those of an Indian tribe. Against Indians and Spaniards the western settler held loose notions of law; his settled purpose was to drive both races from the country, and to take their land. . . . In the end, far more than half the territory of the United States was the spoil of Spanish empire, rarely acquired with perfect propriety. To sum up the story in a single word, Spain had immense influence over the United States; but it was the influence of the whale over its captors,—the charm of a huge, helpless, and profitable victim.[3]

After the Florida agreement, the forces of "Manifest Destiny" continued their advance; they turned toward Texas and Cuba and immediate tension eased. But its end was still far away. It came only with the final departure of Spain from the Western Hemisphere in 1898. It would be tedious and superfluous to examine the different incidents, episodes, and moments of friction involved. The mention of only a few will suffice: the Monroe Doctrine, directed, to be sure, rather against the nations of the Holy Alliance than against Spain; the López expedition of 1850; Maximilian's adventure in Mexico; the "Virginius" Affair in 1873; the War of the Pacific; and, naturally, the pressing question of Cuba.

The final act of this drama was played in 1898, a date that left an indelible impression on the Spanish spirit. In the history of the United States, after the martial agitation of those years, it has been completely forgotten. It will suffice, to understand the state of mind of defeated Spain, to cite the words with which that country accepted the conditions of the American government upon signing the preliminaries of the Treaty of Paris: "This demand strips us of the very last memory of a glorious past and expells us . . . from the Western Hemisphere, which became peopled and civilized through the proud deeds of our ancestors." [4]

Everyone is familiar with the reaction of the Spanish intellectuals, members of the so-called Generation of 1898, to the disaster. But perhaps it would be appropriate to evoke the melancholy words of a Spaniard reared in the United States and intellectually, if not sentimentally, separated from the country of his origin. I refer to George Santayana and to the lines from his poem "Spain in America":

> As the anguished soul, that gasped for difficult breath,
> Passes to silence from its house of pain,
> So from those wrecks, in fumes of lurid death,
> Passed into peace the heavy pride of Spain,
> Passed from that aching tenement, half fain,
> Back to her castled hills and windy moors,
>
> . . . .
>
> And now within her sea-girt walls withdrawn
> She waits in silence for the healing years.[5]

In this brief résumé of ineludible differences, there is not the least moralizing intent, nor any implicit historical judgment. The struggle for power between declining nations and those burgeoning to national life is as normal and inevitable as any natural phenomenon.

The majority of American historians, from Henry Adams to Charles A. Beard, from Henry Steele Commager and Samuel Eliot Morison to Samuel Flagg Bemis, have studied objectively, and not without sympathy toward the vanquished, the events leading to the disaster of 1898. In addition there is a complete and impartial study of relations between the United States and Spain in the large, three-volume work of Admiral French Ensor Chadwick, who understood clearly the deep roots of the conflict. In the introduction he writes: "This book is the outcome of a study of the causes of the war of 1898 between the United States and Spain. Beginning as a preliminary chapter of the war, it was soon found that these causes were of such long growth and of such intricate character that it was vain to hope to bring them into short compass. . . . The late war was thus but the culmination of difficulties that had their seed in the peace of 1763."

Chadwick is even more specific on the final page:

The war was the final act in the struggle for supremacy between Anglo-Saxons and men of the Latin race in North America, in which Philip, Elizabeth, Drake, Howard, Chatham, Vernon, Wolfe, Montcalm, Washington had, all, a part. The expedition of the Great Armada; the murderous early struggles in Carolina and Florida; the seven years' war that drove France from the American continent, were but acts in the drama the culmination of which, in 1898, left the Anglo-Saxon and the American in Mexico masters of the whole of the northern continent. It was the end of a race struggle which had lasted full three hundred years.

Spanish domination in America, in which there had been much both of glory and of shame, with splendid episodes of heroic endeavor, noble self-abnegation, and great attainment, was to end in the final sacrifice, nobly met, in the sea which had through generations witnessed so many conflicts of the two races.

Though Spain was to lose her American dominion, she was not to lose the good-will and kindly regard of the American people, linked as these are with her by the chain wrought by the great discoverer, and to whom Spain must ever be the land which has made so much of the history of the Western World.[6]

With the advent of the twentieth century, Spain, withdrawn behind her walls and awaiting, in the words of Santayana, "in silence for the healing years," disappears for all practical purposes from the international scene. Until 1936, with the Civil War in Spain, Americans will not again know anything, politically speaking, of a country that had had so much importance in the history of their own nation. Today the military bases are once more establishing a political relationship between the two peoples.

II

LET us now turn to an examination of cultural relations, which are much more extensive than generally believed and about which we possess a rather detailed knowledge in the work of Professor Stanley T. Williams, *The Spanish Background of American Literature.*

Williams, onetime professor of English literature at Yale University, was not a professional Hispanist, and in consequence his work gains in impartiality. He began through an early interest in the travels of Washington Irving in the Peninsula and, after many years of study, finally elaborated what he rightly calls in the introduction "the first complete record of one of the great Continental influences upon our literature." He soon realized the vast and intricate nature of the subject, as well as the complexity and contradictions born of the historic rivalry and stated that "to many Americans Spain and Mexico still suggest vaguely: troublesome neighbors, the unfortunate wars of 1848 and 1898, and political instability. Our historians have solidified the myths by letting us forget that even now the English areas of civilization in the Americas are smaller than the Spanish and Portuguese. In the past Spain ruled more than half of the regions now forming the United States."

Even so, neither the rivalry nor the myths to which Wil-

18

liams alludes prevent an interest in certain aspects of Spanish culture (in many instances greater than that felt for more related ones), as the following words from the same introduction indicate: "This total debt [of American literature to Spain] is less overwhelming than to England, to France, or to Germany, and it is also less significant, at least quantitatively. Nevertheless, for American men of letters the fascination of Spain has in some ways exceeded that of other European countries, hardly excepting England itself." [7]

Of the above there is ample proof in the two generous volumes of Professor Williams' work, with their nearly nine hundred pages of text. We are interested only in giving a succinct account of the many facts and observations that this scholar and other investigators have contributed, attempting simply to indicate outstanding points.

Already in the early colonies an interest in Spanish matters was born of religious rivalry. According to Williams, "hatred of Spain and of all her ways burned deep and lasting in the minds of the English colonists of the seventeenth century on the Atlantic seaboard . . . race, religion, economic rivalry— everything counseled enmity."

Two of the most representative figures of Puritanism, Cotton Mather and Samuel Sewall, began the study of Spanish with the intention of creating proselytes. Sewall wished to use the Spanish Bible for "the bombing of Santa [sic] Domingo, the Havana, Porto Rico, and Mexico itself," and Mather wrote a book on the Protestant religion that he translated into Spanish with, according to him, "a design to send it by all the wayes that I can into the several parts of Spanish America." It was published in Boston in 1699 with the title *La Fe del Christiano en Veyntequatro Artículos,* and I cannot refrain from citing a part of the title page: "Sent to the Spaniards so that they will open their eyes and be converted from darkness to light, and from the power of Satan to that of God." Sewall and Mather wished to establish in Mexico a kind of religious utopia to be called New Jerusalem.[8]

These plans, so nonliterary in themselves, led, nevertheless, to the reading of Spanish authors. Already during the last years of the seventeenth century allusions are found to various writers and books known to the colonists: Bartolomé de las Casas and the earliest chroniclers and explorers; Juan Luis Vives, Diego de Saavedra Fajardo, the *Visions* of Francisco de Quevedo, the *Lazarillo de Tormes*, the *Celestina* and, especially, the *Quijote* of Cervantes which, from the very first, captivated the Americans. According to Williams' comment, "His immediate presence in seventeenth-century America, where we search in vain for editions of Shakespeare, is both surprising and exciting."

As the eighteenth century advances, the number of Spanish books in libraries, allusions in learned reviews, and data on the Spanish world is truly amazing. This has been amply demonstrated by Harry Bernstein in various studies such as *Making an inter-American Mind*[9] or the previously cited *Origins of inter-American Interest, 1700–1812;* or by Edith Helman in her article "Early Interest in Spanish in New England (1815–1835)."[10]

During the century of independence and the Enlightenment the religious factor became less predominant,* and American intellectuals and thinkers, the founders of the nation, turned toward the luminaries of France and England. Nevertheless, interest in Spain showed a notable increase. The abundance of books and authors in private and university libraries is truly astonishing—from Nebrija to Pedro Mexía and the *Amadís de Gaula,* from Lope de Vega and Tirso de Molina

---

* Of course, transformed with other designs, it still persists in the evangelizing activities of various groups in some Hispanic-American countries and even in Spain itself, although after the Civil War in Spain the religious situation there rendered it entirely impossible.

to the *Guzmán de Alfarache* or Ercilla and Jorge de Monte-
mayor, with Cervantes at the head. Authors of the eighteenth
century were also known—Iriarte, Cadalso, Ramón de la
Cruz, Feijóo, Jovellanos, and Isla. From 1734 advertisements
of history books, grammars and dictionaries, or notices by
persons seeking private tutors of the language began to appear in various magazines. A few years later, in 1749, at the
suggestion of Benjamin Franklin, the study of Spanish became part of the curriculum of the Philadelphia Academy, a
city which, partly through the influence of Franklin himself,
was to become a focal point of interest in Spain's language
and literature and the center for varied activities of Spaniards in the United States. In fact, several distinguished
Spaniards, among them the Count of Campomanes, were
elected members of the Philosophical Society, and a considerable number of books and pamphlets were printed in that
city. Beginning in the year 1765, another center for the
publication of Spanish books was Charleston, South Carolina.[11]

John Adams and Thomas Jefferson also took an interest in
the study of the Spanish language, the latter including it in
the courses of William and Mary in 1780 and subsequently
in those of the University of Virginia when it was established
in 1819. In addition to the American Philosophical Society,
other cultural institutions, such as the Massachusetts Historical Society, the American Academy of Arts and Sciences,
and the New York Historical Society showed a very early
interest in Spanish culture and even in the development of
the natural sciences in Spain and Hispanic America. One
scientist taking an interest in the Hispanic world was Benjamin Smith Barton.[12] Another, Dr. Samuel Latham Mitchill
of Columbia College, praised the Spanish naturalists in a
meeting of the New York Historical Society in 1813. He declared that he wished it in his power "to state the particu-

lars . . . for the improvement of American botany made by
the Kings of Spain. There is not perhaps a government upon
earth that has expended so much money for the advancement
of this branch of natural history as that of the Castilian
Monarch." And in a review of the *Political Essay on the
Kingdom of New Spain* of Humboldt, published in the *New
York Medical Repository*, one reads: "Nothing has been a
more trite and erroneous subject of remark than the ignorance of the lazy Dons. . . . This is a miserable and unwor-
thy prejudice. A moderate inquiry will evince that New Spain
has produced a full proportion of respectable observers and
valuable writings. . . . And as to public spirit and patron-
age, it has been manifested in the endowments of learned institutions and in the encouragement of scientific men to an
extent of which no parallel exists in our State of Society."

At the same time, and even before the Romantic fashion,
Spanish themes began to appear in American literature: in
drama, narrative prose, and poetry. Professor F. S. Stimson,
who has studied the question, groups the different themes
under the following titles: "Columbus and the Discovery,"
"The Black Legend," "The Noble Savage," "Peninsular History and Legend," "Quixotism," "The *Comedia*," etc.[13]

After this rapid review, the affirmation of Edith Helman
that "interest in Spanish . . . goes back to the first efforts
of our countrymen toward intellectual independence and
self-expression" seems justified.

During the nineteenth century the panorama became
richer and more varied. This was perhaps the period in which
certain American minds felt closest to the Spanish creative
temperament. The contradictory forces, hostility and attraction, did not disappear, but various factors tended to rein-
force rapprochement. The United States, simultaneously
conscious of its power and of its limitations as a young nation, turned toward Europe and tried to absorb its cultural

heritage. Rivalry with Spain, ever present, diminished with the Florida treaty and the independence of the Hispanic-American countries; the loss of Cuba and Puerto Rico was considered inevitable sooner or later, and, as a concomitant, the end of Spanish hegemony in the Western Hemisphere. Moreover, the heroic resistance of the Spanish people during the Napoleonic Wars kindled the enthusiasm of the Anglo-Saxon world in a manner not greatly different from what occurred during the late Civil War in Spain. The dithyrambs of Southey, Wordsworth, or Byron to the defense of the Peninsula found an echo in the "Public Festival Given by the Citizens of Boston at the Exchange Coffee House, January 24, 1809, in Honor of Spanish Valour and Patriotism," at which Boston's most fashionable poet, Robert Treat Paine, dedicated an ode to the occasion.[14]

With the restoration of absolutism in Spain, the persecution of Valentín de Foronda, a Spanish liberal well known in the United States, where he had been a representative of the Spanish government, as well as the presence of certain émigrés such as Manuel Torres and later Agustín de Letamendi, awakened a degree of sympathy for the liberal cause.[15]

In addition to the above, one must not overlook the interest the United States had in knowing the languages and cultures of the other American republics, and some believed the shortest route to this end lay in a study of the literature and history of Spain. Finally, the intellectual elite of New England, in intimate contact with English, French, and German cultures, received from these the image of romantic Spain, half-Arabic, half-European; land of caballeros and beggars, of rogues and mystics. This was the country that more than any other had kept alive in its ballad literature the popular spirit of a heroic tradition and the spirit of the Middle Ages; the country that, in the theatre of Lope de Vega, and particularly in that of Calderón de la Barca, had become the incarnation of the sense of honor; and the country that, in the characters of Don Quijote and Sancho Panza, had created the two loftiest symbols of human duality and conflict. It is immaterial whether or not we accept this image of Spain today. For our present purpose it suffices to explain the origin of a great wave of interest in Spain, especially among the intellectuals of New England, a wave that later was to envelop other groups. This is the tradition of Irving, Ticknor, Prescott, Bryant, Longfellow, Lowell, and Howells. Williams sums up effectively the significance of their devotion to Spanish culture: "For Ticknor and Prescott it meant a prolonged consecration; for Irving an enrichment of his imaginative life; for Longfellow a gateway into the world of European romantic literature; for Bryant an inward solace; for Lowell a spiritual experience in one or two writers; for Howells an invigorated critical life; and for Bret Harte the arresting of a neglected tradition." [16]

But these authors, studied in detail by Williams since he considers them the principal interpreters, are only one part of the picture, perchance the least significant. Even discounting historians specializing in Spanish subject matter— Prescott, Bancroft, Moses, Bolton, Chapman, Merriman, and many who have continued this tradition—travelers and translators, and certain early critics—Alexander and Edward Everett, Caleb Cushing, Edward Wigglesworth, Jared Sparks, or a bibliographer like Obadiah Rich—I believe the thing of most importance is the total volume of interest in Spanish culture: contact with the whole of this culture or with some aspect of it by American writers and intellectuals up until very recent times. From John Adams, Thomas Jefferson, or Richard Henry Dana to Ralph Waldo Emerson, Henry Adams, or Irving Babbitt; from Herman Melville, Mark Twain, Nathaniel Hawthorne, Edgar Allan Poe, or Walt Whitman to Ezra Pound, Hart Crane, Gertrude Stein, Archibald Mac-

Leish (the author of *Conquistador*), William Carlos Williams (penetrating commentator of the *Poem of the Cid*), or Thornton Wilder (such a devotee of the art and theatre of Lope de Vega), many are the noted names in the annals of American literature who have felt the attraction of Spain— an attraction in some cases limited to a fleeting contact, in others an influence of more lasting character.

Americans have been interested especially in Spain's past: in Cervantes, Calderón, Lope de Vega, its picaresque literature; in mystics like Saint Theresa and Saint John of the Cross. However, certain authors of modern and contemporary Spain have occasionally enjoyed a passing, if not particularly significant, popularity. Thus we see that Howells, for example, was a great admirer of Galdós, Valera, and Palacio Valdés and, in general, considered Spanish realism a more desirable model or artistic creed than the French or Russian varieties.

During the present century the sale of Blasco Ibáñez' books reached unheard-of proportions, and in the theatre not so long ago Benavente, Martínez Sierra, and the Quintero brothers were among the best known Continental dramatists. Unamuno and Ortega y Gasset enjoy a limited circle of admirers, and few European poets and dramatists have experienced the success of Lorca. Let us not overlook either the great influence of Pío Baroja on two writers who about 1920 opened new horizons to the American novel: John Dos Passos and Ernest Hemingway.

If we look for a moment at the plastic arts, we note the enduring attraction exerted by Velásquez, Goya, and El Greco; the intense, although fleeting, enthusiasm for Zuloaga and Sorolla some thirty or forty years ago; and we see how today, among the most admired painters in pre-abstract, cubist, or surrealistic art, Juan Gris, Joan Miró, Dalí, and especially Picasso, outshine those of any other country. We should not be deceived by Picasso's attachment to the Parisian school, because in few artists do we see greater evidence of the Spanish creative impulse, even after his fifty years of residence in France. Nothing is farther removed from the sense of intellectual order that characterizes the French than the ability to detect the most arbitrary forms in reality, as does Picasso. Gertrude Stein, who knew him well, sees this with complete clarity:

Well, Don Quixote was a Spaniard, he did not imagine things, he saw things and it was not a dream, it was not lunacy, he really saw them.
    Well Picasso is a Spaniard. . . . The things that Picasso could see were the things which had their own reality, reality not of things seen but of things that exist.[17]

Perhaps what lies behind this interest we have been discussing is the peculiar nature of the Spanish temperament, its duality, so difficult to reduce to formulas. But let us not forget that there is also a romantic and idealistic vein in the Anglo-Saxon tradition and in the American. We shall return to this point later on. For the moment let us indicate only the strange coupling of disagreement and attraction, of admiration and perplexity, of liking and, shall we say, scorn, or at least an air of superiority, reflected in the majority of American books—history, travel, interpretative essays—about Spain and the Spaniard.

Already in the eighteenth century, Joel Barlow, author of *The Columbiad* and *The Vision of Columbus,* painted the Spaniards with Milton's words on Satan: "majestic, heroic, and perfidious."

The first somewhat alarming impressions that George Ticknor had of Spain in 1818 soon turned into a great admiration for the Spanish people. "There is," he remarked, "more national character here, more originality and poetry in the popular manners and feelings, more force without barbarism, and civilization without corruption, than I have found anywhere else." And he is not speaking here of the educated classes but of the great populace, the common people, whom he declares to be "the best he has known in Europe." He doubtless found in them the same quality that Dana observed in the Hispanic Americans of Juan Fernández Island, "who wear rags with the air of grandees and who maintain their dignity unruffled in every mischance of this mortal life." [18]

The experiences and reactions of Longfellow, a few years later, were not going to differ from those of Ticknor,* his predecessor in the professorship at Harvard University. He went to Spain most unwillingly, and then only after acceding to the repeated insistence of his father. He had prepared himself, rather, to go to Germany and Italy, and was determined to give up the idea of learning Spanish and visiting the Peninsula: "That country is filled with all the horrors of a civil war—It is as much as one's life is worth to visit it— We get most terrible accounts from every quarter." When finally he decided to go, the change in his attitude was radical: "I know that it will give you joy to know that I am pleasantly situated here. . . . I find much more frank and sincere feeling of kindness toward me as a stranger here in Spain than I found in France. The outside of the Spanish character is proud, and on that account at first a little forbidding. But there is a warm current of noble sentiment flowing round the heart." [19]

He remained in Spain eight months, and it is revealing to observe through his letters and diaries how the country, the land, the customs, the works of art, and the people gradually won him over. His progress in the language was rapid, and,

---

* First Smith Professor of the French and Spanish Languages and Literatures at Harvard University. (Translator's note.)

as had been the case with Ticknor, he developed a lifelong interest in Spanish literature, and especially, as was natural, in its poetry.

The experiences of Ticknor and Longfellow were repeated with few exceptions in the cases of many other Americans, as is apparent from the considerable number of travel books on Spain: from those of Washington Irving or Alexander Slidell Mackenzie (author of A Year in Spain) to the more perspicacious ones of Waldo Frank and Georgiana Goddard King in our century. According to Williams there are hundreds of such volumes, and among them some written by at least a half-dozen authors of first rank. I shall omit details and examples. The majority have little that is new or interesting to add and ordinarily repeat the consecrated clichés. There is nothing more insipid than the observations of the majority of travelers who believe, nevertheless, that they have made world-shaking discoveries. And particularly those who write about Spain rarely fail to express a sympathetic astonishment over the country, a fact that does not prevent their saying things quite offensive to the sensitive Spaniard. A prime illustration of this is the book of H. C. Chatfield-Taylor, The Land of the Castanet, that moved Valera to write a caustic and rather amusing rejoinder.*

The interesting thing here is the persistence of contradictory impressions and reactions. One might cite as a typical example the Castilian Days of John Hay. An intelligent and educated man, without any previous interest in Hispanic matters, he wrote an equally intelligent book, in which he brings together the impressions of a long residence in Spain as a diplomatic representative. It is not always possible to discover in his pages, at times delightful, at times biting, "the magic and romantic scenes" to which reference is made in the prefatory note to the revised edition of 1890. But not

* See pp. 52–54.

infrequently, on the other hand, we find in them "the sincerity that the author tried to preserve upon speaking of things that awakened in him, with identical force, affection and aversion." He was only rarely guilty of romantic sentimentalism, he was a most astute observer, and, if in what he saw and in his way of reflecting it he was not overly flattering, he was doubtless sincere when he said, "I hope not to have been inopportune in speaking of a people whose art, literature, language, and character move me to the highest admiration, and in whose midst I made friendships that I preserve among the most cherished memories of my life."

The ambivalence is a permanent one. Attraction toward Spain exists, but it is repressed by a mysterious quality of the Spanish mind which, according to Henry Adams—a good friend of Hay—"no American ever would wholly comprehend."

Irving Babbitt must have been referring to this when, in his essay "Lights and Shades of the Spanish Character," he spoke of "that something Spanish in the Spaniard that causes him to behave in a Spanish manner." Naturally something similar could be said of other national temperaments—of Frenchmen, Italians, or Germans—but it is unquestionable that the Spaniard's peculiarities reveal aspects farther removed from the mentality of the average American than do some other nationalities.

It seems apparent, after this rapid review, that, notwithstanding the hostility between the two cultures—the one inclined toward the social and the technical and the other mystic, anarchical, and individualistic—attraction and curiosity are undeniable and that we are dealing with a more than fortuitous phenomenon. Williams speaks insistently about the charm that Spanish history has had for American historians, and to explain it he uses concepts and phrases such as "the fascination of Spain," "the mysterious qualities of the Spanish mind," "the intrusion of the past into the present." And he reaches the conclusion that his compatriots "did not find stimuli of exactly that nature in the history of other European nations."

The experiences of writers, historians, and artists is doubtless repeated in the less conscious relations of visitors and tourists. As an ordinary thing they do not see beyond the picturesque and the superficial. However, if they are at all discerning, they are not long in realizing the complexity of the "Soul of Spain," the title, it may be noted in passing, of an extremely penetrating book by the Englishman Havelock Ellis.

We could accept as valid certain of Professor Williams' conclusions:

At times these American writers had glimpses of an individualism whose central intensities they could not emotionally share. . . . But they neither comprehended nor mirrored the Spanish whole, this blend of animal and mystic, this Spanish "Man of Flesh and Bone."

This Spanish passion for the separate man . . . creates individuals, each inviolate, each in himself a walled city, yet each a part of Spain.

This extreme belief in the untrammeled development of the individual, of all his physical, intellectual, aesthetic, and spiritual impulses, still confuses us, especially when we see this idea thriving in a country in which ordinary freedoms, in our naïve sense of the word, hardly exist. This dream of honor, of beggars as kings, this *personalismo*, triumphant in the midst of oppression, of political inequalities, and even of anarchy—this we have been able neither to absorb in our thinking nor transfer to our literature.

There is a chasm. . . . That it exists is, in the light of our undying curiosity about Spain, both amusing and tragic. . . . A few writers seem to have entered into this enigmatic "Spanish mind." We recall how the mysticism of the Spaniard reached recesses in the spiritual lives of Bryant and Longfellow, and we might guess that Poe was not without sympathy for the Spanish attitude toward death. In particular, we have observed a sustained response in our literature not merely to Cervantes' fantasy and humor but to his piercing, universal wisdom.

It should not be forgotten, however, that Williams made a special study of the nineteenth century and that the historical and realistic complexion of that period was not the best suited for an exploration of the intimate realities that seem to concern him.

Quantitatively, interest in Spain decreases during the twentieth century, at least among the most outstanding figures of American culture; but, on the other hand, as a sort of compensation, we have a few profound and distinguished interpretations. Hemingway, for example, whose debt to Spain deserves a thorough study, has, in his work *Death in the Afternoon* and in certain stories such as *The Undefeated* (more than in *The Sun Also Rises* or *For Whom the Bell Tolls*), understood well certain of the fundamental traits of Spanish character: how to face failure, and especially death, with grace and dignity; and how to be a man in the fullest sense of the word, an understanding of man and his predicament that Havelock Ellis has defined with incisive exactness: "Spain represents, above all, the supreme manifestation of a certain primitive and eternal attitude of the human spirit, an attitude of heroic energy, directed not chiefly towards comfort or towards gain, but towards the more fundamental facts of human existence." [20]

There are, in addition, two books about Spain by foreign authors which I would not hesitate to place among those revealing the deepest understanding of that country. I refer to *Virgin Spain* by Waldo Frank and *Heart of Spain* by Georgiana Goddard King. In both of these works, written in 1926, we see the influence of the urge for self-definition, the "search for the Spanish soul" so characteristic of the men of the Generation of 1898 (Ganivet, Unamuno, Menéndez Pidal) and a little later of Ortega y Gasset and his generation. Each of these books succeeds in avoiding the hackneyed clichés and immerses itself in what Frank calls in the subtitle of his work "The Drama of a Great People." Both see the unity and the moral reserves beneath the apparent contradictions of "the Spain that sleeps and dreams," according to Frank's phrase: "The once furious and unleashed elements of the Spanish soul have been woven into this counterpoint of rest: they make a quiet music."

Frank also spoke of the awakening of Spain, perhaps without suspecting the fury of that awakening during the following decade. Space does not permit us to comment on the development of his interpretation but only to point out the suggestive way in which he comes to grips with the problem. His interpretation is based in part on the intention to refute two myths: "The world," he says, "nurses two myths concerning Spain. The first that she is decadent . . . the other . . . that Spain is romantic."

Frank's vision of Spain is suggestive, poetic, and philosophical. That of Georgiana King is more restrained and tied to facts—impressions on art and on the spirit of Castilian cities and villages—but equally fresh, original, and anti-romantic. She says: "Indeed the key to Spanish character and to a large part of Spanish literature and thought may be found in a fact that has rarely been appreciated in all its consequences: the actual predominance there of practical reason over the speculative."

This statement, after all, agrees with what other American observers were able to discern whenever they succeeded in forgetting the romantic image of my country: the solidity of the Spanish character, "the steel of the Spanish mind and temperament" that Mark Twain and Howells perceived along with the Spaniard's deep-rooted realism.

We have made no reference to the two most evident aspects of our subject: the great development of Spanish studies in the colleges and universities of the United States during the last forty years and the direct contribution of Spain to the very existence of two-thirds of the country. Spain discovered and explored a vast section of what today is United States territory, and Spanish culture, language, and customs still persist, although in a somewhat hybrid and primitive form, among part of the population of the Southwest. But, although we should not forget these facts, it has seemed more interesting to us, upon comparing the two cultures, to approach the subject from another standpoint.[21]

III

O F perhaps less interest from our point of view is the other aspect of the question: how Spaniards have reacted to the culture of the United States and what they have received from it. This is a subject of less breadth, and one to which much less study has been dedicated, since old cultures ordinarily influence the new and not vice versa. Actually, virtually nothing has been done toward its study. Consequently, although we have limited ourselves to a general investigation, we have analyzed with some thoroughness the reactions of a number of authors, especially those from the nineteenth century.

It should be noted that we are disregarding the old chroniclers who penetrated what is now United States territory, as well as the work of various professional historians who have made documentary studies of certain subjects in the area of historical and diplomatic relations between our two countries. The mention of a few names will suffice for our present purpose: Fernández Duro, Hernández Díaz, Serrano y Sanz, Gómez del Campillo, Yela Utrilla, Conrotte, Ramón Ezquerra, Pérez Hervás, Rodríguez Casado, etc. Although their studies would be germane to a comprehensive investigation, they throw virtually no light on the specific topic that interests us: how Spaniards have responded when in *living contact* with Anglo-Saxon culture in the United States, or what the reflection of that culture is in the world of values.

According to José de Onís, the only one as far as we know who has investigated the subject on the basis of original sources, the American colonies were but little known to Spaniards and Hispanic Americans prior to 1776, when they began their war with England. He cites various documents and historical works of limited interest prior to 1800.[22] I believe, however, that, independently of these, we can point to the presence of the United States in Spanish literature for the first time in the novel *Eusebio,* by the ex-Jesuit Pedro Montegón. This work was published in 1786 and enjoyed a great success in its time until its proscription by the Inquisition. Inspired by Rousseau's *Emile,* it tells the story of a Spanish youth, Eusebio, who, a shipwrecked orphan on the coast of Maryland, is adopted by a family of Quakers in Philadelphia. When in the end he returns to Europe with his teacher, Mr. Hardyl, the reader is shown the contrast between the luxury and atmosphere of struggle characterizing Europe and the simplicity of American life. Hardyl, who turns out to be a Spaniard also, explains that he chose Pennsylvania as a refuge suitable for freedom of conscience and as a spot propitious for the cultivation of the natural virtues. Although before dying Hardyl abjures and is reconciled with Catholicism (the Inquisition made such a denouement advisable), one sees here clearly the reflection of an idea or topic current since the eighteenth century—the United States as the country of freedom of conscience—and of another that has lost its significance, but which persisted until almost the end of the nineteenth—the ideal of the natural and virtuous life that culminated in Thoreau.

Among the first Spaniards to have direct contact with the United States were the diplomats such as the Marquis of Casa

Yrujo and Valentín de Foronda and political agents such as Juan Mariano Picornell, Manuel Torres, and José Alvarez de Toledo. Of all the above, the one of greatest interest for our purposes is Foronda, who became very closely identified with American life, as his relations with Jefferson show. He was even made an honorary member of the American Philosophical Society in 1804. In addition to his papers and dispatches, he left some *Apuntes ligeros sobre los Estados Unidos de la América Septentrional,* where one detects, along with the exaltation of liberty and American institutions, another idea identified with the vision of the United States: economic prosperity as the fruit of freedom.[23]

Enthusiasm did not so blind Foronda as to prevent him from warning Cevallos of the danger that the rapid increase of "these republicans" posed for Mexico. Detectable here, on the one hand, is a suggestion of the same fears expressed in the Count of Aranda's "secret memorandum" of 1783; on the other hand is a specific, although tenuous and involuntary, warning of what with time will become the subject of the "Yankee Peril."

The negative view, conceived in the light of the expansionist ambitions of the new nation and combined in some instances with an objective, exact, and documented impression (which was obviously partial at times), is now explicitly seen in the *Memoria sobre las negociaciones entre España y los Estados Unidos de América.* This was the work of Luis de Onís, *chargé d'affaires,* and later the first minister of Spain in the United States. He spent ten years there in intense diplomatic activity and was Adams' opponent in the above-mentioned negotiations leading to the sale of Florida. An interesting figure in the history of Spanish diplomacy, he concerns us only for his impressions of the country. We shall consider this for a moment because his book is, in fact, the first in Spanish about the United States and because it is not readily accessible. As will be the case with other travelers, we note in Onís an ambivalent reaction of admiration and rejection—a phenomenon paralleled in the experience of Americans with Spain, although, to be sure, differently motivated in his case.

Onís says, for example: "The outlook of the United States . . . is indeed glorious and admirable; their progress in only forty years of existence; the rapid increase in their population, their wealth, their physical force; and their resources seem large when one compares the short period in which they have acquired this power and splendor with the long centuries other nations have required to raise themselves to a thriving and respectable condition."

But then he immediately states that they are not a new nation but, rather, a people who have benefited from the enlightenment of Europe (an obvious fact); that they are a nation destined for early destruction through conflicts in their federal system (and this is much more doubtful), through incompatibility between their executive and legislative branches, and through their materialism and sensuality. According to Onís, sensuality is especially apparent in the South. "The whites appear to decrease rather than increase in those states. This can only be attributed to their use of strong drink, and to their voluptuous and corrupt way of life. They commonly mate with Negroes and mulattoes and scorn marriage. They are little given to work, are presumptuous, vengeful, and cruel to their slaves."

People from the northern states impressed him as more industrious and less corrupt, but basically he felt that all of the country was dominated by an "extreme and exaggerated desire for luxury" and by "the blind determination to engage in overly risky business speculations and enterprises." This had resulted in the destruction of the great fortunes and a considerable erosion of public wealth. He is discussing, in short, one of the first depressions or economic crises that will be repeated following periods of prosperity—an economic phenomenon that Onís analyzes with great insight.

Onís was far from being a Tocqueville; rather, he was a reactionary, irritated, moreover, by ten years of diplomatic haggling. Even so, his reports and memoranda on the country—population, geography, politics, business, etc.—can still be read with a certain interest, and not a few of his political, social, and psychological observations reveal marked perspicacity.

He is naturally alarmed by the threat that the new country poses for his own and never tires of denouncing what for him, an old European, was the intolerable sense of superiority of this young nation: "Americans now believe themselves superior to all the nations of Europe, and that it is their manifest destiny to extend their domination immediately to the Isthmus of Panama, and later to all the regions of the New World."

These two concerns became obsessions with him. Let us examine another quotation:

The Anglo-Americans view all nations with scorn or contempt, admiring only the English, from whom they are proud to be descended. . . . Their vanity and arrogance reach extremes that can scarcely be imagined. They consider themselves superior to other men, and view their republic as the only establishment on the face of the earth founded on a great and solid basis, beautified by wisdom, and destined one day to be the most sublime colossus of human power and the marvel of marvels of the entire universe.

Concerning expansionist plans and the absorption of Spanish possessions, he says: "The United States have elaborated their plan with wise and seasoned reflection; they follow it coolly in the manner of England; regardless of administration they do not alter it one iota, unless through the pressure of events and treaties their relations and interests have changed." And in the face of this, Spanish weakness makes him sad and indignant for he says that "our weakness made it clear to the United States that they could attempt with impunity to annex to their territory those possessions of the monarchy that most suited their desires."

In the light of the expansive force of the United States, Onís foresaw the inevitability of the conflict with great clarity. Although fully conscious of the ultimate futility of his efforts, he worked with determination to contain the avalanche, and his zeal induced Carlos Pereyra, the Mexican historian, to speak of him as "a brilliant Americanist."

For his part, the English translator of the *Memoria* took proper note of its contradictory character and the reasons behind this: "The reader of the following pages will soon find reasons for considering them a really astonishing product: he will realize that they contain a singular mixture of the most obvious calumnies and the most exaggerated praise of our country. . . ." And the principal reason for this contradiction was the way in which Onís had been blindly accused in Madrid for having gone against the interests of Spain in signing the treaty, "through fear or from partiality toward the Americans." [24]

As particularly germane to our subject, we note in this first attempt at political rapprochement on the part of a Spaniard (leaving aside the briefer and more fruitful one made by Foronda) that ambivalence toward the United States, commonly found, moreover, in the majority of Europeans and in large measure still persistent in our time: on the one hand, there is admiration for the country of freedom with an unbounded future, the hope of humanity; on the other, consciousness of a threat to civilization from a materialistic nation scorning the highest forms of spirituality, impelled by its mania for imperialistic expansion and economic supremacy. Both attitudes will be repeated afterwards with only slight variations, and, as is always the case with history, both contain elements of truth, but not the whole truth.

Years later, in 1841, an interesting and extreme echo of the negative attitude is to be found in Blanco White's journal: "I am reading *Abdy's Journal* on the United States, a work that convinces me of the existence of a moral illness in that nation. Antipathy toward the Negroes and their most distant descendants borders on madness. Despite my great love of liberty, I would not live in that Union, precisely because I love it. The United States live under the tyranny of ignorance and prejudice. I would prefer to live under a sultan. The mob is the worst tyrant, because it lacks individuality." [25]

Following the *Memoria* of Onís, a liberal émigré, Miguel Carmona de Nenclares, wrote some *Observaciones acerca de los Estados Unidos del Norte en 1834*, as yet unedited.[26] And during the same period Don Ramón de la Sagra, naturalist, economist, resident of Cuba for some twelve or fourteen years, author of numerous works on economy and the natural sciences, spent "Five Months in the United States." Under this title he collected his impressions in perhaps the most complete book on that country by a Spaniard, since until the present time few are able to compete favorably with it. We have not seen the Spanish edition but have examined the French.[27]

It is not without interest that immediately after the publication of Tocqueville's classic work, *Democracy in America,* a Frenchman, enthusiastic over the new country, stopped writing his own book and decided, rather, to translate the travel journal of la Sagra, a relatively obscure Spaniard, for reasons that he explains in his preface: "I was surprised by the novelty and importance of the documents found therein, by the candor of the narration, and the originality of the observations."

The translator was not exaggerating. The journal describes the author's impressions on the following itinerary: New York City, navigation of the Hudson River, and a visit to the whole of northern New York State as far as Buffalo and Niagara Falls; then on to Boston, returning through Connecticut for departure from New York. Everything interests la Sagra, and he sees everything with unprejudiced eyes: with exactness, objectivity, and a certain enthusiasm—a rare accomplishment in travel literature. He notes, among other things, the atmosphere of the cities, the country's railroads, theaters, customs, institutions (scientific, educational, and charitable), newspapers, the freedom of the young ladies, and the beauty of the women.

But perhaps the thing that affords the best measure of la Sagra's attitude was his belief that the new democracy was a model worthy of imitation by the divided Spain to which he was soon to return, after his long absence, with plans for reforms. He states: "With the idea that what Spain needs is *education* and *reforms* . . . my purpose in this book is to recommend primary education, and the moral reform of the Spanish people." And, farther on:

Perhaps some men of exaggerated opinions in the two camps will find the doctrines I have examined in the United States but little compatible with their principles: the liberals, for example, will be alarmed over the severity of the moral and religious obligations in force in this country; the absolutists in turn will be scandalized upon seeing me praise the customs and religious convictions of a nation of republicans.

But I say to the former that they will seek the happiness of the Spanish nation in vain elsewhere, and to the latter that they should imitate the conduct of the sons of freedom if they would make religion appealing and respectable.

At least three nineteenth-century Spanish writers of some note had personal relations with the United States: the poetess Carolina Coronado, the poet and diplomat Gabriel García Tassara, and the diplomat and novelist Juan Valera. Rather than to a direct knowledge of the country, the interest of the Romantic poetess in the United States was owed to family circumstances: she married Horatio J. Perry, Secretary of the American Legation in Madrid. He informed William H. Seward, Secretary of State in President Lincoln's cabinet, in a letter of 1863 that "no one had rendered greater service to the Republic [than his wife] in most critical circumstances." She enjoyed a firm friendship and maintained a literary correspondence with William Cullen Bryant, who translated her poem "El pájaro verde," and in her "Oda a Lincoln" she feels herself identified with the native country of her husband and of the Great Liberator, whom she proclaims "the hope of America."

> Porque también yo soy americana
> aunque el manso Guadiana
> me vió nacer en su abrasada orilla
> como flor destinada
> para ser transplantada
> y dar a otro hemisferio su semilla.*

The case of García Tassara is a strange one. He spent ten years in the United States, from 1856 to 1867. These were, indirectly, important years in relations between the two countries: those of the War between the States, the abortive annexation of Santa Domingo, the Franco-Spanish intervention in Mexico (from which Spain, fortunately, withdrew in time), the War of the Pacific, and the recrudescence of the Cuban problem. Not only does he seem to have carried

---

* Because I too am an American/although the placid Guadiana/saw my birth on its sun-baked shores/like a flower destined/to be transplanted/and give its seed to another hemisphere. (Translator's note.)

out his assignment in these matters with tact, but to judge from what his biographer Mario Méndez Bejarano says of him (the only one who has treated the question, although not in great depth), with his clear sense of the unity of language and culture he was extremely effective in promoting harmonious relations among his Hispanic-American colleagues. In the tense situation caused by the invasion of Mexico and the War of the Pacific, he strove to assuage resentment. One of his Hispanic-American intimates, the Ecuadorian D. Antonio Flores, paid him the following tribute:

> Those of us who have had the honor of being friends and companions of Tassara in the capital of the United States can appreciate the desperation of that noble soul, who dreamed frenziedly of a great confederation of Spanish-speaking peoples, with Spain at the head.
> He wished to apply to our race, on a larger scale, the theory of nationalities that fascinated and ruined Napoleon III. If his efforts were not blessed with success, neither were they sterile, nor did they fail to be properly appreciated in America.
> The waters of the Pacific would not have been reddened with blood, nor would a senseless war have broken out after forty years of peace, to open wounds anew and revive the painful memories of the War of Independence, if a Tassara had occupied in South America the place entrusted alternately to a Salazar y Mazarredo, to a Pinzón, or to a Pareja.[28]

Despite what this judgment suggests, which is considerable, the subject seems to have interested no one except Méndez Bejarano, who has devoted a comprehensive study to the poet.[29] The cabinet in Washington requested Tassara's transfer, which was effected by the government of Madrid, but both President Andrew Johnson and Seward paid public tribute to his tact and sagacity.

Regarding our special interest in him, we know little or

nothing of what he thought of the United States. It is only in a letter to Ríos Rosas in 1858 that we find a not very original judgment, an echo, moreover, of a common attitude among Europeans: "Meanwhile I shall remain here as long as I can do so with dignity, charging myself with electricity against *these bombastic people, the most vainglorious, that is to say the least glorious and the vainest in the universe. When the time comes I shall leave, and they will hear things from me all the more harsh because no one esteems their admirable qualities more than I."

This letter reveals further that Tassara saw very clearly— a rare trait among the Spanish diplomats of his time—the importance of the United States in the complex relations of Spain with its American family: "Well, from here, from the lion's mouth . . . I declare that in the United States not only do we have nothing to lose, but a great deal to gain: the restoration of our race, our own restoration in the world." [30]

In addition to his diplomatic activities in Washington, it would seem that Tassara was otherwise quite engrossed in love affairs, nothing surprising in the Don Juanesque poet. Of the various presumptive liaisons, Méndez Bejarano gives a detailed account only of Tassara's relationship with young Magdalena Goddard, which says little for the fidelity of the former sweetheart of the Cuban poetess Gertrudis Gómez de Avellaneda.

We know absolutely nothing about Tassara's interest in American literature, and it is doubtful whether this field held any attraction for the translator of Camões, Horace, Virgil, and Shakespeare. On the other hand, the much briefer stay of Juan Valera is more revealing as regards literary relationships and judgments on American letters. It should be noted that this minor phase in the diplomatic peregrinations of the author of *Pepita Jiménez*—Naples, London, Rio de

Janeiro, Dresden, Saint Petersburg, Frankfurt, Brussels, and Vienna—has only recently attracted the attention of certain critics and biographers: Cyrus C. De Coster, José L. Cano, and Carmen Bravo Villasante.[31] We shall rely on them, particularly on De Coster, for a detailed account.

Valera arrived in the United States in January of 1884 and left in the spring of 1886. Unlike Tassara, he did not distinguish himself in his diplomatic mission, either by his efficiency or his enthusiasm, although as a matter of fact little if anything could have been done to clear up the only question pending between the two countries—Cuba. De Coster cites the doubtless well-founded opinion of John W. Foster, United States minister in Madrid. The latter had said that "those who knew him well at home predicted that he would not make a successful Minister, as he did not have the disposition or business capacity to master the intricate and annoying questions involved in our relations with Cuba, notwithstanding his social gifts and his literary talents. The prediction proved correct."

The published correspondence does not afford us as coherent and explicit a picture of his reactions as do his letters from Russia, but it is adequate. One senses that he is hesitant to relate in detail his impressions of a country that never succeeded in interesting him. This reluctance, however, has its explanation. He was sixty years old, and had wished neither to be separated from his family nor to leave Europe. Moreover, his innate skepticism had sharpened with the years, while his taste for life's pleasures, although it had not disappeared, had been notably tempered.

Thus, even in his first letters, the perspicacious observer, so apparent in his Russian letters and in others, is glimpsed only rarely. Later, near the end of his mission, he experienced one of the great sorrows of his life, the death of his oldest son, Carlos, who had remained in Spain with his mother.

This plunged him into the depths of despair. And to this was added the suicide of Katherine Lee Bayard, the young woman—daughter of the Secretary of State—who had fallen hopelessly in love with the old Spanish diplomat. Manuel Azaña is right when he speaks of the "terrible moral crisis" that Don Juan experienced in Washington.

And, despite all of this, the correspondence still contains enough information for us to get a rather exact idea of Valera's reactions, not overly original to be sure, but frequently conveyed with that jaunty nonchalance, bordering at times on cynicism, with which he was wont to express himself. We note clearly the customary duality of European judgments of the new country. The first impressions are very favorable: "All this is beautiful: the people are kind and hospitable; the women are stunning, a fact to which I am not indifferent, although I am old, for one's eyes rejoice at beholding beauty; and this capital is most charming, full of gardens and great trees, and ample lawns that will make it a paradise once spring is here."[32]

Similar, and even more encomiastic judgments are repeated from time to time; but, generally speaking, the unfavorable, frequently the insulting, note predominates: "The cooking is very bad here and this grieves me"; the politicians "are either oafs or thieves, and not infrequently both." Or, more explicity:

Men here are very rude and not very amiable. They are all engrossed with business, a euphemism for knavery and robbing to get money. Here, ordinarily, people are such rascals and thieves that Spain by comparison seems the abode of saints.

The rich fools, not in the business of making money, set themselves up as scholars and men of letters, and write very dull things.

Many of the young ladies and women are blue-stockings, assert that they know even Latin and Greek, and are apt to blurt out a Latin phrase when you least expect it. Other young women are amazons and travel alone, carry whips, and own dogs and horses. All of them ride, go to the theatre, and even travel with gentle-men.[33]

Even so, most of his opinions are favorable to the American woman, although he is occasionally shocked by her freedom. When he learns of his possible transfer, his feelings, as is the case throughout all his correspondence, are contradictory. He feels that they are depriving him of economic advantages: "I can see for sure that they are going to take this plum from me." And in another letter he says, "I want to go, and at the same time I want to stay." In the end, however, the desire to return to Spain prevailed.

Aside from Carolina Coronado and her relations with Bry-ant, and the various friends and correspondents of Ticknor and other Hispanists (scholars for the most part), Valera, un-less further research proves otherwise, seems to have been the first Spanish writer to have a direct contact with the litera-ture of the United States. He met various authors and cor-responded with some of them; he translated poems of Lowell, Story, and Whittier and published them in *Canciones, ro-mances y poemas*. The translation and criticism of certain authors came much earlier than this, as can be seen in John De Lancey Ferguson's work, *American Literature in Spain*, which we shall discuss later. For the moment we are con-cerned only with personal relationships.

In his article Cano assembles various facts gleaned from the correspondence published by De Coster and from Va-lera's article "Poesía angloamericana," from which we are reproducing a few sentences only by way of contrast to the latter's ordinarily more negative views: "There are a con-siderable number of poets here, and some of them are nota-ble. The best at the moment are Holmes and Whittier . . . ; people read here much more than in Spain . . . ; they could

form an army from their pretty and elegant poetesses alone;
many are eminent. The names of only a few of their distinguished poets have reached Spain. . . ."

Literary information and impressions are also to be found
in Valera's correspondence with Menéndez y Pelayo. Moreover, the fact that he was a well-known man of letters
awakened the interest of Americans, one of the results of
which was the translation of his novel *Pepita Jiménez*. In
general it was well received, but certain adverse criticism,
provoked by what reviewers considered the scandalous nature of the work, occasioned the following outburst in a letter
to his nephew José Alcalá Galiano: "The newspapers speak
about it [*Pepita Jiménez*] a great deal: some like it and others
do not. Now, since these rascals are so hypocritical, they have
begun to call my novel immoral, impure, scandalous. Perhaps
this will increase its sale. The Appletons allow me ten per
cent. But despite my earnings . . . I resent deeply that this
godless, money-loving riffraff should mistreat me and offend
my ingenuous and passionate heroine, only because she gives
herself to Don Luis, as though Yankee girls never gave themselves to anyone." [34] In these ill-tempered though witty
words, as in many others, are echoed the frequently unfounded scorn and prejudices of the European.

The judgments to be found in certain of his critical essays
are more seasoned, and of greater importance. In a majority
of instances these are commentaries on criticism hostile to
Spain, exacerbated as the conflict of 1898 draws near. The
aggressiveness and ignorance of the works he comments
on justifies Valera's reaction. Even so, one is able to discern here, along with irony, an effort to be just and objective, in recognition of the intrinsic value of American culture.

In the essay entitled "Sobre dos tremendas acusaciones
contra España del angloamericano Draper," he discusses the

book by J. W. Draper, *History of the Intellectual Development of Europe,* in which, among other things, it was said of Spain that "it has been her evil destiny to ruin two civilizations, Oriental and Occidental," and "in America she destroyed races more civilized than herself." In the same essay he replies in even more vigorous language to the article by Clarence King—"perhaps the most ferocious of the anti-Spanish writers"—"Shall Cuba be Free," published in *The Forum.*

According to Valera the sole purpose of both writers is to awaken in the United States hatred and scorn for Spain in favor of the Cuban rebels. He defends Spanish culture with those arguments which, since the polemics of the eighteenth century, have been used in combatting the Black Legend, ridicules certain aspects of United States culture, and reveals his scorn for Messrs. Draper and King; on the whole, however, the tone is moderate.

Not overlooking the question of slavery, and rebutting the accusations of cruelty leveled at the Inquisition, he does not forget the burning of witches and sorcerers in Europe and in the American colonies: "Wherefrom I am inclined to suspect that in all America, dominated by Spain during the sixteenth and seventeenth centuries, there were not as many victims of the Inquisition . . . as were sacrificed in the United States, while still colonies, for the crime of witchcraft." [35]

And his attitude toward the Cuban problem is not devoid of a certain nobility. He of course defends the rights of Spain, as was to be expected, and even thinks the emancipation of Cuba impossible. This, however, does not prevent his saying finally:

Above and beyond patriotism there lives and breathes in us the love of caste or of race. First of all may Cuba continue to be Spanish; but should she cease to be, may she soon become, to the glory and satisfaction of the former mother country, a great, highly cultured, and flourishing republic. Then Máximo Gómez, for example, whom now we would shoot or hang without scruple, in compliance with an onerous obligation, would stand resplendent—the object of our applause—in the ranks of the eminent liberators; he could be placed on a level with Simón Bolívar and George Washington, and have statues and monuments like theirs.[36]

The essay "Los Estados Unidos contra España" is more serious, complete, and sincere. Strictly speaking it is a denunciation of American conduct in the "lamentable Cuban war." Valera feels the grief of Spain, and a bitter note appears in these pages. In the end, however, his moderate, comprehensive spirit prevails. In a way, and independently of the warlike circumstances under which they were formulated, certain of Valera's concepts could be considered typical of the clash and attraction of the two cultures.

He complains of the "harsh, ferocious manner in which the American senate has insulted Spain"; he considers a rupture of relations inevitable and lays it to the machinations of the politicians, noting: "one must bear in mind that in that great Republic the politicians are not ordinarily the most esteemed, best educated, and most sensible people"; and that the majority "in that *great nation* neither think nor feel as do their violent politicians." Farther on he alludes to "the stupid Monroe Doctrine" and, in the area of culture, does not deny the great accomplishments of the United States, although he emphasizes that these are simply a prolongation of English and general European culture. Europe is still the guiding hand of Western culture: a reasonable opinion in Valera's time and one which, as we shall see later, still continues to be, perhaps with less justification, that of the majority of Europeans. Valera says:

Everything the Yankees have thought, invented, or written may well be a brilliant appendage; but it is no more than this, an appendage of English civilization. It may well be a very shining appurtenance, but it is no more than that. The nucleus, the focal point, the moving force, all that still illuminates and urges humanity forward in its path, is to be found in Europe; it has not passed to America, nor need we fear that it will. The torch of learning and intelligence, the authority of knowledge, the ship's rudder, and the sceptre of intellectual sovereignty have been in Europe for three hundred years.[37]

A little farther on, in an outburst of wounded patriotism, he asks that war be declared, although without great hope of victory: "Rather than suffer so much ignominy and such a great fall, since all hopes of an honorable peace have vanished, let us declare war on the United States; let us do this with courage and, although our final victory may seem a miracle, let us have faith and trust that the age of miracles is not past. . . ."

At the end, rising above the senseless patriotism that had engulfed both nations, he proclaims his high regard for the many admirable things he had seen in the United States:

And I, despite myself, cannot exclude the United States from my love of the human race, a country where there were, and indeed still are, men and things that I find agreeable: elegant and inspired poets such as Longfellow, Lowell, and Whittier; a number of thinkers, not very original but discreet and clever, such as Emerson, an imitator of Carlyle; various historians, although not particularly profound, pleasant and enjoyable to read except when they talk about their own affairs, because then they are very boring; a few amusing novelists and, especially, men of such keen inventive talent that at one moment they shine like Edison, using electricity in countless useful and amazing devices, or at the next produce the sewing machine, a contraption that leaves me dumbfounded whenever I observe it. Moreover, I admire the beauty, the talent, and the refined culture of American women. They are the most valuable and certain guarantee that if the Monroe Doctrine were ever put into strict practice, and there were established a divorce between the Old and the New

World, the inhabitants of the latter would not again dress in feathers and skins, sacrifice human beings to idols, or once again eat each other. I admire Niagara Falls, the richness and prosperity of the United States, the magnificence and splendor of its great cities such as New York, Boston, and Philadelphia; the ease and convenience of railway travel there; the friendliness and hospitality of Yankees toward foreigners—this when self-esteem does not blind them, and when they do not get the idea that foreigners are greatly inferior to them, because then they are most unfriendly and uncharitable. Consider the poor Chinese, sorely put upon because they work for paltry wages. In short, as far as I am concerned, in spite of the way they have treated us, I would like to see us make up, respect and come to love one another instead of fighting.

He feels that if the war is lost an annoying matter will have been liquidated, but if a miracle occurs and the Americans are defeated, perhaps it will be a boon for them. He further says:

And if we are victorious, since everything is possible with Heaven's blessing . . . then the Yankees will greatly mend their ways, because their pride, their greatest shortcoming, will be humbled; and I, although burdened with illness and advanced years, shall take pleasure in seeing the Yankees kinder and more peaceable, less harsh and insolent with us, disowning the foolishness of their Monroe Doctrine, and extending to us, as they should, the hand of friendship devoid of bitterness.[38]

A different tone, since here Don Juan returns to his customary irony in polemical matters, is seen in the article "El país de la castañeta." In addition to its wit, its special interest for us stems from the fact that it notes, with great discernment and precision, the key to the differences—religious rivalry—and takes cognizance of the exact but paradoxical fact that in the relations of the two cultures praise at times can be more biting than censure. He is commenting on the book

The Land of the Castanet, by H. C. Chatfield-Taylor. We shall limit ourselves to a few quotations:

We find an insult even in the title. It is as though a Spaniard were to write a book on the United States and, without remembering Washington, Franklin, Lincoln, Grant, Emerson, Poe, Channing, or Whittier, and many other illustrious personages; without mentioning its remarkable and beautiful women, its great cities, its monuments, its wealth and prosperity, the expanse of the Hudson and the Mississippi, and Niagara Falls, recalled only the many pigs that are raised and slaughtered in Chicago, and entitled his book *The Country of the Pig.*

From the book as a whole it can be inferred that Mr. Taylor wishes to treat us favorably; but, in spite of himself, the deceptive Protestant prism through which he views us causes him at one moment to slander and insult us involuntarily and candidly, and at the next to heap on and against us prophecies, prognostications, and opinions that I consider absurd.

He says, for example, that we, in our pride, have a worse opinion of the Yankees than they of us. The only thing that has been done in Spain by way of rebuttal is to rejoin with a series of insults that I find in the worst possible taste. These have been in answer to others a thousand times baser and more depraved in nature that senators, representatives, self-proclaimed serious writers and journalists of the Great Republic have directed against us in the past, and of which we continue to be the object today.

Taylor himself, who tries, wishes, and aspires in good faith to be our apologist, from the second line of his book calls us indolent and cruel. To accuse us of fanaticism and superstition, as Mr. Taylor frequently does, scarcely offends us, for this accusation is so unreasonable and unfounded that it can only strike us as ludicrous. Were we to compile statistics on the number of persons executed, burned, or murdered for religious reasons, the number on the list of the sentimental and most pious Anglo-Saxon race would be double or triple the number on ours, despite Torquemada and all the inquisitors.

. . . Let us end this article . . . declaring that Mr. Taylor's book is very readable despite the few defects we have noted and that, if we try not to be touchy, we must recognize that what he has to say against us springs from prejudices difficult to eradicate from the soul of a foreigner; and that basically Mr. Taylor either praises us or tries to do so, and that on almost all the pages of his book he demonstrates a very sincere and warm friendliness toward us.[39]

In various other parts of Valera's work one finds comments on American authors such as Emerson, but these add nothing to the opinions on the country that we have enumerated.

Were one to investigate our subject systematically, he would discover here and there a considerable number of further allusions. Men like Giner de los Ríos, Pi y Margall, or Castelar felt a great admiration for certain political aspects of the United States, either the federal system, democracy, or religious liberty. Castelar goes so far as to proclaim that only beyond the Atlantic Ocean is democracy possible, and, in a rhetorical outburst in his famous speech on the abolition of slavery, he does not hesitate to pair Washington and Lincoln with Christ. And so he concludes his exhortation of the deputies, in which he urges them to vote the bill into law, telling them that when they go home they can think: "Yesterday obscure, today we are immortal; we are members of the race of Christ, of Washington, of Spartacus, and of Lincoln because we have fearlessly pronounced the word *liberty.*"

In another framework and as an indirect reflection, it could be noted that two novelistic characters of Galdós, whose roles are to demonstrate a lack of prejudice and the renovating spirit of enterprise, have been formed in the United States: Agustín Caballero of *Tormento* and Pepet of *La loca de la casa.* And other characters in certain of his dramatic works intend to emigrate to the United States, fleeing Spanish struggles in search of a free future.

The reverse of these positive, commonplace evaluations— the United States, home of freedom, etc.—is to be found in another equally current platitude—the United States, that recognizes no value save money—of which the following dialogue of Campoamor serves as a good example:

How does Mr. Rodríguez expect me not to look with scorn on a social doctrine whose economic catechism, written by an American, can be reduced to these five questions and answers?

What is life?
A time in which to earn money.

What is money?
The aim of life.

And man?
A machine for earning money.

And woman?
A machine for spending money.

And children?
A seed producing machines to earn and spend money.

To this must be added that, in contrast to Castelar's view of the United States as the only country where democracy was possible, Campoamor believed that it was "the one country in the world where only slavery was possible." [40]

Another important aspect of our inquiry would be the influence of American literature. In the face of former and present-day scorn for the United States, based on the view that it is a country devoid of creative capacity and talented only for commercial ventures, we are surprised not so much by the richness of its literature, little more than a century and a half old, as by the fact that this literature has had, almost from the beginning, a considerable influence in disdainful Europe. No one, for example, can doubt the importance of Poe, by way of Baudelaire, on the renovation of poetic sensibility, from which a great part of European poetry of the last hundred years comes.

On the question of the influence, or at least the diffusion, of American literature in Spain during the nineteenth century, there is a book we have seldom seen quoted except by specialists in the matter of literary relations between the two countries. This is the work of John De Lancey Ferguson, *American Literature in Spain*.[41] Although somewhat out-of-date, it affords a good survey of the subject, as well as detailed information on the most important authors: Irving, Cooper, Poe, Hawthorne, Longfellow, Prescott, Emerson, and Whitman. According to Ferguson, translations of American authors began to appear around 1830. At that time, or a little later, James Fenimore Cooper was one of the most translated writers, even competing with Sir Walter Scott in the number of translations and in esteem of readers and critics.[42] Gil y Carrasco, for example, in a long review of the work of Eugène A. Vail, *De la littérature et des hommes de lettres des États-Unis d'Amérique*, says of the works of Cooper that they "are for his country a source of glory and pride, and because of their truth, simplicity and good taste will always be quoted as models of good narrative and lively interest." A little later he does not hesitate to rank him with Scott and place him in the first echelon of "original writers." Gil voices other interesting opinions on American literature, still inferior in his judgment to that of Europe. He thinks that a man like Robert Fulton represents the new civilization better than any writer or philosopher, although he believes the country's literary future will be "undoubtedly brilliant."

Irving, Hawthorne, Longfellow, Prescott, and Emerson were also translated and praised, as were lesser figures— Louisa May Alcott, Thomas Aldrich, Ethel Beers, Bret Harte, Harriet Beecher Stowe, and others. The same was true of scientists like Agassiz or Audubon, historians like Bancroft, and sundry personalities like Phineas Taylor Barnum and Andrew Carnegie. Mark Twain, a figure nearer to our time, was quite popular. But the two most fruitful influences were doubtless that of Poe in the first instance and later that of

Whitman, both already thoroughly studied by, among others, John Englekirk and Fernando Alegría. The most representative Americans are, in order, Franklin and Jefferson. Strangely enough Ferguson cites only one book about Lincoln. As for magazine articles, he has collected one hundred and sixty-four, without pretending to exhaust the material. The majority are no more than an echo of what was being said and thought in Europe, especially in France, but they do contain, nevertheless, certain important observations.

Especially notable in this connection are the articles of Angel Guerra (José Betancort) on Poe and Whitman. In the first, for example, the author defines the unity of the United States as follows: "An alluvial country, composed of the detritus of other nations and races, it has attained a unity of character and a rectilinear spirit that it has been able to transform into a solid nationality." To him the cohesive element was "a commonly-shared desire for spiritual freedom and independence, already burning in the first immigrants." And he continues:

The same dominant trait is to be noted in the artistic and intellectual life of the United States. The inflexible morality of the Puritans has always predominated. In this, one finds the ideal of its thinkers and the inspiration of its poets. . . . Its oldest writers . . . like Cotton Mather are theologians rather than men of letters. When the artistic rebirth occurs, its writers do not deviate from this rectilinear spirit . . . until they attain the splendors of the loftiest art and culture. All of their intellectually eminent men, from Franklin to Emerson, are moralists; as are also their poets, from Longfellow to Whitman; or their novelists, from Irving to Hawthorne. Even in our day one can detect that moralistic basis underlying the humor of Mark Twain.

As valuable criticism one could also cite that of Cebriá Montoliú, translator of Whitman and Emerson and author of the book *Walt Whitman: l'home i sa tasca,* but we feel that what has already been said is sufficient to give an idea of Spanish interest in American literature from its earliest times.[43]

Ferguson, like Williams, was cognizant of the influence of historical changes and politics on literary relations, and makes a résumé, notable, like so many passages by American historians, for its objectivity and understanding of the contending forces:

> In Spanish admiration for American literature . . . a distinct change in attitude is to be noted with the passage of three-quarters of a century. About 1830, when translations of our authors first began to appear in the Peninsula, the United States was regarded by the oppressed and hunted Spanish Liberals as the embodiment of human freedom and of all that is best and noblest in government.
>
> The Mexican War, with its exhibition of aggression and rapacity on the part of the idealized North American republic, must have shaken Spanish faith in the integrity and magnanimity of the successors of Washington.
>
> The unfortunate aptitude of Americans for rubbing the Latin races the wrong way does not conduce to mutual respect and esteem even when there is no intentional offense on either side, and when American contempt for Spanish character and conduct culminated in the discreditable war of 1898 we need not be surprised to find our manners and institutions no longer commanding the wholehearted admiration of the Spanish people. When his works were first translated, Fenimore Cooper was praised because his writings seemed typically American; today, Spanish critics tend to admire Poe for the very reason that he is not typically American, and Walt Whitman because he represents the old American ideal from which his fellowcountrymen have long since fallen away. This change in attitude offers food for thought.[44]

During the last fifty years, relations intensified, and the panorama widened enormously—to such a degree that to examine it in any detail, however summarily, would require considerable space. We shall limit ourselves to a few indications in the form of an index or guide.

The reasons for such intensification are obvious: the internationalization of life, the greater facilities of communication, the development of what one might call the traveling spirit—the great political and social upheavals with their attendant displacements. To this must also be added the great increase of interest in Spain and its culture. As a result, many Spanish writers and intellectuals, either through brief contacts or longer periods of residence, have come to know the United States. Let us recall a few names, without any pretense to complete exactness: essayists, dramatists, and novelists, such as Benavente, Valle-Inclán, Maeztu, Blasco Ibáñez, Pérez de Ayala, Martínez Sierra, Madariaga, Camba; almost all of the poets, such as Juan Ramón Jiménez, León Felipe, Moreno Villa, Lorca, Alberti, Larrea; and the most brilliant figures of philology and history, from Ramón Menéndez Pidal and his immediate pupils—Américo Castro, Navarro Tomás, Onís, and Solalinde—to the younger intellectuals of a later generation—Dámaso and Amado Alonso, Salinas, and Guillén, in their dual roles as poets and mentors, Montesinos, Casalduero, Centeno, Lapesa, Lloréns, Julián Marías, Ferrater Mora, Francisco Ayala, Francisco García Lorca, Juan López Morillas, and Ernesto DaCal—followed by a still younger group, formed in part in American universities. The list is impressive and could be augmented without including scientists, politicians, economists, diplomats, journalists, and simple emigrants. And in a more systematic inquiry one should not forget the fleeting contact of Ortega y Gasset or the very special case of George Santayana. Santayana was an American by virtue of education and professional activity, a citizen of the world through his philosophical posture and that radical uprooting he defines so well in the first pages of *My Host the World,* but a Spaniard to the end through citizenship and perhaps also through sentiment. Ortega y Gasset visited the United States very briefly in 1945, but before this he had already written a few typically penetrating pages on the American scene.

It would be interesting to see in each instance, even in the cases of those who have written on the subject only in a cursory fashion, how this new world affects their learning or their poetry in a negative, hostile, or friendly manner. How, for example, it influenced those pages of Maeztu on the reverential feeling for money; the poetic evolution of León Felipe, who found his thundering, prophetic, and Whitman-like voice in the United States; the deepening of Américo Castro's historical view, or, and here the influence may be more subtle, the last poetry of Salinas and Guillén; the search for, and the discovery of, the new poetic conception of Larrea; or the philosophical ideas of Ferrater Mora. In each case the influence, either as affirmation or reaction, is completely different and may come through unexpected channels, but perhaps it would be worthwhile for someone to study it carefully. Such an inquiry would reveal the complicated function of the contribution made at this stage of the world to Hispanic sensibility and European culture (under whose aegis all the above figures are formed) by the reality of the United States—a reality fertile or disturbing as the case may be, but unquestionably powerful.

But, forsaking the area of conjecture, it can be noted that these contacts produced a series of books we shall not stop to examine, except to point out very rapidly this or that suggestive characteristic. For example, we have the exuberant enthusiasm of Blasco Ibáñez who, in his *Vuelta al mundo de un novelista,* entones, like a man of action, a song to the ironlike energy of New York—"a work of giants . . . extraordinary and fantastic"—as though it were another planet, where men had conquered the laws of gravity, "a city of miracles, mother of a powerful race of magicians, creator of the most stupendous inventions of our century, poets of action, workers for whom the word impossible does not exist . . . a city that has conquered the night."

This spontaneous exaltation contrasts with the penetrating humor of Julio Camba who, in *Un año en el otro mundo* and later in *La ciudad automática,* has probably given us, in caricature, in his ironic and exaggerated manner, one of the most profound interpretations of the United States ever made by a Spaniard. As is so characteristic of Camba, everything appears slightly ridiculed or reduced to the absurd. And, as is the case in his other works on Germany, London, France, and Spain itself, he has been able to penetrate the essential values of a strange and even comic reality, which is difficult for a sophisticated European to do. Thus along with what would seem to be a negative attitude, we note his full realization of what the United States represents for civilization in the crisis of our century. For example, he sees that the nation's economic power and its young soldiers (whose tramplings and elbow jabs he had endured in the New York subway) were going to rescue the Allies from the serious predicament in which they found themselves in 1917 (this is repeated during the Second World War), and he forebodes the perhaps disquieting possibilities that might develop in the heart of the picturesque country of the "gum chewers," the "incredible drugstores," and the ostensible "equal opportunity." He states in the introduction to his first book: "I believed, finally, that machines were being developed in the United States more intensely than taste and feeling, but with no idea of substituting the latter. Now I am beginning to think the opposite. When I am firmly convinced of this, the United States will strike me as a country of infinite possibilities: the country, quite simply, from which nothing short of a new humanity can arise."

This was a double-edged prediction which seventeen years later, in *La ciudad automática,* a Camba now completely disillusioned about progress (it is not to be forgotten that he started out somewhat anarchical) sees fulfilled, but which inspires not the faintest enthusiasm in him. "Only New York," he says, "has succeeded in embodying our period, and probably this is the real reason why the great city simultaneously attracts and repels us in such a powerful manner. It attracts us because one cannot live divorced from time, and it repels us because of the great stupidity of the time in which it has been our lot to live."

Another discerning capturer of national nuances, the poet and painter José Moreno Villa, assembled in his *Pruebas de Nueva York* (1927) a collection of very personal impressions on the city. As such, these do not deal with conventional subjects, but, even so, they reveal the inevitable duality of viewpoint in the evaluation of American life as seen by a European. On the one hand we find praise for leisure as preferable to frenetic action directed only to earning money: "Why money, if at forty I am part of the ruin I see about me? I prefer to enjoy life and communicate its greatness and complexity to others, although I have no dollars; I prefer to die from beer than from jolting; I prefer to be a nobleman with an abundance of free time and subsisting on crumbs than a worn-out laborer with gold." On the other hand we note the confession of an admiration that the majority of Europeans ordinarily hide: "The European recoils and puts himself on guard against Yankee influence; but this influence is to be noted in a multitude of things belonging to today's cosmopolitan life, not only material, but moral and social as well. No good European wishes to see his deep, long, and complicated civilization replaced by another that strikes him as defective and superficial; but at the same time there is no doubt that every good European feels a confessed or unconfessed admiration for the Yankee's gay imperturbability in the face of the difficulties of everyday life."

It is a pity that Salvador de Madariaga has never given us his complete interpretation of the American, as he did in the case of the French and the English. His book *Americans* has a quite different purpose: it is a plea for world unity. Even so, in this and in other of his works one can find traces, together with a certain amount of biting criticism, of opinions and observations outside the beaten path.

And now closer to us we have the book of Julián Marías, *Los Estados Unidos en escorzo,* which, amidst the mass of commonplaces that every writing traveler ordinarily accumulates, sets itself, and accomplishes, the difficult task of seeing things simply as they are: the task of capturing reality and, what is more important, the small, everyday realities— how people live, play, work, and feel. And this, as it should be, without attempting meaningless comparisons.

As early as the first chapter, "El europeo en los Estados Unidos," Marías indicates the prejudices that cause many visitors to leave without understanding anything. To such individuals there should be added, of course, the countless café and plaza orators who, with no more information than what they have gleaned from the movies, and on the basis of a few tendentious facts, allow themselves to scorn the United States today; this because of a complicated mixture of resentment, ignorance, and perhaps a justified bit of disenchantment vis-à-vis a democratic faith which, owing to very complex reasons, does not always act in a way completely consonant with its principles.

The first prejudice, according to Marías, consists in believing that one "already knows what the United States is."

He continues: "The other assumptions about the country are the principal components of this foregoing idea and could be summed up as follows: lack of originality, cult of the modern and the colossal, uniformity, vulgarity. And the inevitable consequence that closes the chain and joins the initial assumption is lack of interest." All of which leads him to the following commentary: "I fail to understand how intellectuals, who would have given their right arms to see the beginning of the Roman Empire, can fail to be interested in the formation of one of the three or four most astonishing historical creations that man has been privileged to see until now and which, through rare good fortune, is taking place before our very eyes."

To his capacity for interpreting social phenomena theoretically, Marías adds that of describing such phenomena exactly. The result is an intelligent and honest book—a not very frequent combination these days. In our opinion it is one of the best for learning how the American lives the less spectacular phases of his existence which, after all, are the most authentic.

Marías, a Spaniard and a European, does not fail to perceive, along with national differences, certain devaluations in American life, some of which are alarming. But he is also aware that this subversion of values, at times imputed to the society of the United States, is not so essentially an American trait as a hallmark of our time, and perhaps more alarming and serious in Europe itself. If in some instances it is more apparent in the United States, this is compensated for by a "health" rare today in the Old World. In fact, to develop this idea he devotes an essay to "The Health of American Society," and in this he sees a basis for hope. "As I am not a professional pessimist," he writes, "I believe that health too is contagious. And I hope that, in the near future, the irradiation from that portion of humanity found in the

United States may prevent or cure ugly eruptions in other areas."

The impressions and interpretations of traveling writers and essayists should be rounded out with the view of the poets (a more difficult task): the delicate and contradictory view—smoke and gold, black and rose, light and shadow—of Juan Ramón Jiménez in his *Diario de un poeta recién casado* or, later, in the *Romances de Coral Gables;* the surrealistic and apocalyptic vision—geometry, mechanical jungle, anguish—of Lorca in *Poeta en Nueva York;* the ironic vision of Pedro Salinas; the prophetic and hopeless vision of León Felipe as revealed in his imprecations.

And, although the next book we would mention is of a different nature, one should not forget the recent publication of an important work, the *Historia de la literatura norteamericana,* by Concha Zardoya, doubtless the most versed among us in this subject. In addition to the book's very complete information, it reveals an awareness of the currents that have shaped the American spirit, interpretative discernment, and many accurate judgments.

In all cases there is apparent the clash and attraction of these two cultures that history has set face to face in the New World and which, in this way or that, continue to confront each other in the clash and attraction of the two Americas.

On the other hand, the influence of every aspect of life in the United States, from the literary and the artistic—theater, fiction, poetry, movies, music—to that of social habits, is dominant today in Spain as in most of the world. Meanwhile, the factor of political power continues, as has been the case in other periods, to provoke contradictory reactions. Apropos of this, witness the fact that with the concession of military bases or the constant demand for aid, it is not a little paradoxical—although on the other hand quite natural and understandable—that when American influence is at its height, we should note in Spain, as in the rest of Europe, the disquieting inclination to defame the United States systematically, as though it alone were responsible for the evils and dangers of the world situation.

IV

AFTER this rapid review of historical and literary relations, I should like to conclude with certain general
considerations.

At first glance, and if we accept literally the opinions of
the uncultured American, and perhaps also, I regret to say,
of some cultured ones, it would seem that the two civilizations we have been comparing are actually at opposite poles
from each other. Let us sum up these opinions:

According to them, one civilization, Protestant in origin,
represents the complete triumph of modern thought, the
incarnation of the rationalistic, economic, scientific, and
technical ideals of the Western world during the last two
centuries. The other presents the image of a backward, indolent, superstitious people, at times cruel, at times picturesque
and half-oriental, situated on the border of Europe. The
latter has been the enemy of all progress since the days of
the Counter Reformation, and Spain's role as leader in certain moments of European civilization, or as the discoverer,
explorer, and colonizer of the greater part of the New World
has been either forgotten or falsified. Rarely, with the exception of one or two names, is there any recollection of the
literature or rich artistic creation of this nation. Its contribution to history is ordinarily limited to the Inquisition and its

cruelty, a cruelty no greater and perhaps less inhuman than that which at one time or another has been practiced by other dominant races and nations. Lest it be thought that I exaggerate, I recall such words as hate, scorn, and the like used by the most impartial American historians as descriptive of the generally shared attitudes of their less objective compatriots when the latter discuss Spain and her traditions.

To this image there could be added the assumption that while the United States is indebted to other European countries—England, France, Germany, and the Italy of the Rennaisance—it owes nothing to Spanish culture. And even today, when they look to the nations of America beyond the Rio Grande they feel constrained to adopt a civilizing attitude and bring them the blessings of democracy, education, technology, and free institutions—all those things of which they were deprived through their Spanish heritage.

Far be it from me to ridicule the excellent intentions of such a program or to deny that the Hispanic peoples have a great deal to learn from the United States. But, by the same token, I do not share the equally oversimplified and unjust view, prevalent among Spaniards and other Europeans, that the United States is the land of a crude and materialistic people, devoid, amidst the splendor of their wealth and technology, of all the graces of true civilization, and for whom the measure of everything rests entirely on economic values.

No, fortunately for everyone the facts are quite different from the distorted picture conveyed by such oversimplifications. I hope that we have demonstrated clearly that the forces of attraction working between the two nations have been at least as powerful as those of dislike and estrangement. Contact between the two cultures has been much greater than is generally believed. Many American travelers, historians, and writers, and among them some of the most representative, have known and esteemed Spanish literature and art; on many occasions they have done justice to Spanish history, even in instances of conflict with their own country; and not infrequently they have demonstrated a profound understanding of the best elements of the Spanish character. I believe facts justify Williams' assertion that "for American men of letters the fascination of Spain has in some ways exceeded that of other European countries, hardly excepting England itself." I would go so far as to say that in many cases, notwithstanding the common prejudices, Americans have been more appreciative of Spanish values than the majority of Europeans, with the possible exception of the English, who after all belong to the same tradition.

Spaniards also, strange as it may seem, have felt an instinctive friendliness toward the American, although, like all Europeans, when speaking of the United States they assume an air of superiority and repeat the customary platitudes: pride, aggressiveness, lack of culture and refinement, materialism, etc.

As a conclusion to the foregoing remarks it might be useful to examine a few suggestive ideas.

1. There may well be present in the American and in his national character the mark of certain Spanish traits, without his even suspecting it.

2. Whether such is the case or not, and notwithstanding all the differences, there are certain similarities between Spaniards and Americans that would account not only for the "fascination" of which Williams speaks but also for that paradoxical congeniality we were discussing at the outset.

3. Spain, or more properly the Hispanic world and its culture, can still have something to offer Americans.

When two cultures, one old and one newly emerging, come in contact, it would indeed be surprising if no vestige of the former remained on the newer of the two, which, on displacing the other, cannot help absorbing certain of its elements. The particular forms of Spanish culture and life or, more properly speaking, of Mexican life, that American explorers and colonizers found in the West were without any doubt elemental and remote, coming as they did from zones far removed from the center of influence. Even so, I am convinced that, unbeknown to the new settlers, these cultural forms left some trace on them, later to be incorporated in the national character.

I am certain that no Spaniard or Mexican would recognize as authentic the romantic-popular image of Hispanic California and the Southwest with its synthetic patios and supposedly Spanish architecture; its short-jacketed "caballeros" and ranchers, its mantilla-clad ladies and young women, its simple mission "padres," or its guitar-playing young men, but we should not on that account scorn their significance. They are artistic by-products of a literary tradition that, from Bret Harte and Helen Jackson to the greater artistry of Willa Cather, form a part of the American heritage.

Moreover, Harold W. Bentley, in his work *A Dictionary of Spanish Terms in English*,[45] mentions a large number of words used occasionally by American writers and furnishes a list of some four hundred that have found a place in the English language, especially in the Southwest. We recognize that there is no surer sign of cultural interrelations than the adoption of words.

Sometimes, half jokingly, I tell my American friends that they would be surprised to discover that certain of the myths and symbols they consider typical of their character are of Spanish origin. It would be interesting to analyze how the Anglo-Saxon and Spanish traditions have fused in the supposedly so American image of the western hero and his world in literature and in the movies. We should not forget that, trivial as the subject may seem, this is the image of the hero that children and many adults admire and that it constitutes the popular representation of the American for foreigners. What are the components of that image? A rare mixture of violence and banditry or disregard for the law; of romantic worship of the virtuous woman and the conquest of the dissolute; of a personal and individual sense of honor, an inclination to take justice into one's own hands; and, especially, the affirmation of *manliness* as the supreme value. Although some of these traits may be found in every frontier culture, they show a strange affinity with certain Spanish attitudes, while nothing similar is to be seen in the tradition of New England or in the early southern colonies.

One aspect of the above is the clearly Spanish origin of the greater part of the folkways of the cowboy, with his equivalent in many countries of Spanish origin—the *gaucho*, the *llanero*, or the *vaquero*. To complete the picture we could add the importance of the rider, the man on horseback, as a type and the survival in the West of a form of folk literature, the ballad, accompanied by the guitar, and perhaps a remnant of the old Spanish ballad collections and of the Mexican *corrido*.[46]

I suggest that the foregoing ideas contain more than enough elements to arouse the curiosity of some ingenious essayist.

Making an implicit comparison between the Spanish and the Anglo-Saxon characters, Américo Castro has observed that in English one does not say explicitly "I go," but rather "I'd better go," or "I am afraid I must go," trying to hide the "I," the first person. And he relates all this to an observation by Carlyle: "The negation of being, the nullification of being. This is still the greatest wisdom that God has revealed to us on earth." This denial of being, of the person, is still a very pronounced trait of American psychology, particularly noticeable in the people of New England. However, it is counterbalanced by an opposite tendency: the powerful affirmation of the "I," of the being, of the individual, in gesture, language, and attitude, quite common in the American of our time.

Moreno Villa, in the chapter "Examen de apariencias" from his previously cited book *Pruebas de Nueva York,* made some very perceptive observations, accompanied by drawings, about a certain masculine type he had seen in New York City. He spoke of his suit, his loud necktie bedecking a protruding chest, his bearing, his frank and direct look, and the special way he had of pulling his hat down over his eyes or slanting it to one side. And he detected certain slight signs of arrogance and ostentation that reminded him of the Spanish sporting toughs of the lower classes, a probable remnant of the Spanish rowdy of long ago. It is possible that Moreno Villa found his models in Times Square or at Fiftieth and Broadway (not particularly representative locales), since the image he caught, not very different from some the movies have popularized, would have to be considered the negation, or at least the reverse, of the traditional Anglo-American, so silent, so circumspect, almost timid. In any event, the noisy and aggressive American, a product of the urban melting pot, is also a part of the national reality and must be taken into account for a complete characterization of this national type in his great complexity, a complexity no less, despite powerful unifying forces, than that of any other people.

From the outset we have been suggesting the existence of a mutual attraction between Americans and Spaniards whenever they come in contact with one another; an attraction based perhaps on a rapport impossible to understand at first glance, if one takes into account the great differences between the two cultures and the almost permanent conflict in which they have lived. But the proof of this affinity, nevertheless, is amply demonstrated in the books and judgments of numerous authors.

How can this phenomenon be explained? For reasons difficult to analyze, I believe that Americans have a dual nature, oriented toward opposites, as do, although for different reasons, the Spaniards. In both we have the practical man and the dreamer; the ambitious man who is eager for material riches and the crusader who is guided by a religious, moral, and idealistic instinct that makes him wish to save the world. Whether it be for the glory of a Catholic God (*ad majorem Dei gloriam*)—as was the case with the Spaniard of the sixteenth century—or for democracy, it does not matter psychologically. And the pioneer who opened and organized a vast continent was not too different from that most typical of Spaniards, the conquistador. It is not easy to separate in either the insatiable hunger for gold and the impulse toward idealistic adventure. Extremes meet. Perhaps in no other country does one find such a consummate example of this fusion of Sancho Panza and Don Quijote (i.e., of the practical and the ideal), which would explain the continuous attraction that Cervantes has had for American men of letters.

I recognize that all of this is mere generalization, that analogous parallels could be drawn between other peoples of the universe. But I am convinced, nevertheless, that my thesis does not lack a foundation. Various Spanish writers, José Ortega y Gasset, Claudio Sánchez Albornoz, and Federico de Onís, among others, have written about frontier culture. Their contentions could be applied with equal validity (allowing for differences of time, place, and tradition) to modern America or medieval Spain, and to the Spain of the period of the discoveries and the conquest of the new continent. Perhaps here could be found the key for understanding the parallel I have drawn. Let us recall, moreover, that many American authors have suggested the similarity. For Mark Twain and Howells, among others, "there appeared to be a definite kinship of mind between the practical American and the earthy Spaniard." Lowell noted that the English as well as the Spanish possess "a sense of humor" and are "inclined to gravity." Howells speaks of "a strange affinity between the Anglo-Saxon mind and the Spanish mind; "The two races," he explains, "brought the romantic drama to its highest perfection . . . and the same comic vein seems to run in both people, so widely differentiated by origin, by language, by religion, and by polity."

And Gertrude Stein expressed the same idea paradoxically, as was to be expected of her. She says "that americans can understand spaniards. That they are the only two western nations that can realize abstraction. That in americans it expresses itself by disembodiedness, in literature and machinery, in Spain by ritual so abstract that it does not connect itself with any thing but ritual." [47]

Another friend of paradox, Miguel de Unamuno, saw the Spaniard torn between two extremes, exhibiting a realism attached to objects, to things in their stark materiality, and an extreme idealism, wedded to concepts in their utter abstraction.

Perhaps, as we indicated in the beginning, what both the American and the Spaniard are seeking, in their peculiar individualistic ways, is the meaning of the whole man; what Unamuno called "the man of flesh and bone" rather than the typically European rational or aesthetic man. Which means that in both peoples the inner impulses of personality are more ethical than intellectual.

Jacques Maritain, in his *Reflections on America*, considers the United States—a country, according to him, badly understood today by the majority of Europeans—especially endowed to accomplish the new ideal of what he called in a previous work an integral humanism. In such a search, the United States, like the rest of the continent, has to transform, as it has been doing until now, the best of what each culture of the Old World can offer.

What can the United States expect from Spain? Américo Castro clarified this in a lecture entitled *The Meaning of Spanish Civilization:*

> But if Germany is "Wissenschaft" and France is "clarté," what is Spain? The fact that we do not have a ready formula is very significant. The reason is that, for a Spaniard, living is always an open problem, and not a solution, to be confined in a slogan. To live or to die are for him equivalent points of departure which today, less than ever, cannot be considered an impertinence. Today it seems sure that only those countries able to face death will be able to survive. The best part of Spanish civilization is to be found in its religious, moral, and artistic achievements. . . . According to a Spanish saying, one must do things: "with all one's soul." A drama of Unamuno bears the title: "Nothing less than a whole man." I believe that any contact with Spanish civilization will pave the way for a new and fruitful humanism.[48]

There is, in addition, another fundamental reason why Spanish culture has deserved and continues to merit the attention of Americans. Even if we relegate Spain to the past, one day or another the United States will have to fully accept the fact that its destiny is indissolubly tied to that of the balance of the hemisphere. Only when it comes to know thoroughly the Hispanic roots of that world will it be able to bridge the gap and lack of understanding which, despite all efforts and the best of intentions, still separates it from its neighbors. This was what Waldo Frank saw so clearly many years ago. Early in 1917, when he was speaking to Argentine writers on the subject of Spain in America, he said:

I encountered a poor and exiled fragment of that world in the Southwest of my country. I knew nothing of it; I could not speak its language. But I sensed at once that it had something for me; something for my people; something which my world, the proud industrial world, lacked. . . .

It was the sense that *we*, specifically of the United States, in a civilization top-heavy with machines run by machine-minded and machine-exhausted men, needed a new capacity of integration . . . an organic knowledge, which the Hispanic and the Indo-Hispanic worlds appeared to possess.

The second stage of my understanding was that *we* had something . . . which *your* America needed. Later, only later, I was to see the symbol of our being one hemisphere, one America, together. . . .

We shall let these words of Waldo Frank serve as a preamble or prologue to the second half of our subject, one much more controversial and complex—the relations of Hispanic America with the United States.

PART II

HISPANIC AMERICA
AND THE UNITED STATES
Past, Present, and Future

AMONG the catastrophes and extraordinary transformations of this half century, especially accelerated since the Second World War, two great contrary tendencies are clearly discernible. On the one hand we have the division of interests and geopolitical forces, the so-called Cold War, and the emergence of continents like Asia or Africa, until now slumbering or isolated from the mainstream of history. On the other hand we note unmistakable symptoms that the world is moving toward that unity so long dreamed of by all the utopians: not merely a political but a social unity, with the disappearance of classes and castes and, although it is difficult to imagine today, of conflicts of ideas and beliefs. Never have the dialectical contradictions of historical evolution operated with greater intensity or with greater urgency. Not without reason men, and even nations, feel somewhat adrift, as though pulled by unknown and uncontrollable currents. It was some years ago (1935) that Ortega y Gasset diagnosed the malady: "Well, I believe," he said, "that what is happening to Western man is this: he doesn't really know what to do or what to be, either individually or collectively." Disorientation continues and has even grown worse. It would seem today that Western man doesn't know where to go and, what is more serious, where he wants to go.

I

IN this situation, the ancient dispute between Europe and the New World over the direction of Western culture again poses itself with nagging persistence. The alternatives past-future, decadence-progress go back almost to the days of the discovery. Explorers, conquistadors, and settlers sensed confusedly that they were creating a new reality in the virgin lands; humanists and utopians, Erasmus, Sir Thomas More, Montaigne, made all kinds of predictions of a better life, with man freed from want and slavery. Already in 1581 the skeptic Francisco Sánchez, author of *Que nada se sabe* (*Quod nihil scitur*), had affirmed that "the men of the New World are little by little becoming more religious, of keener perception, more learned than we ourselves." [1]

As everyone is aware, the debate was intensified to the extreme during the eighteenth century. If Buffon, De Pauw, and, in a different vein, Hume or Voltaire defended the thesis of the intrinsic inferiority of the American continent, there were others who proclaimed the bankruptcy of Europe and the promise of America. Thus the Abbé Galiani wrote to Mme. d'Epinay in 1776: "The time for the total collapse of Europe and for transmigration to America has arrived. Everything around us falls from rot: religion, laws, arts, and sciences; and everything is going to be reconstructed from the ground up in the New World."

Raynal, so great an Americanist, knew how to reconcile the extremes. His assertions on man and his surroundings did not at all run counter to those of Buffon or De Pauw, but on the other hand he foresaw, after more or less immediate suffering and cataclysms, a better future. The prophecy, although well known, is still of interest, especially in the threateningly critical moment in which we find ourselves today: "If any successful revolution takes place on earth it will come from America. After having been devastated, that New World should flourish in its turn and perhaps rule over the old. It will be the haven of our peoples downtrodden by politics or the victims of war."

However, it is not a question for the moment of the old controversies, studied among us by Antonello Gerbi,[2] but of a living awareness of the promise and worth of America. If after the First World War, when for the first time American armies set out to rescue the European democracies from the German peril, doleful prognostications were lavished on the old continent, during the last fifteen years the conviction of a serious European decline has become a commonplace.

No one can deny that the axis of command has its center in Washington, and the portentous prophecy of Alexis de Tocqueville would seem to have become a reality: "At the present time [he refers to 1835, the date the first part of his book appeared] there are two great nations in the world which seem to tend toward the same end, although they started from different points: I refer to the Russians and the Americans. All other nations seem to have nearly reached their natural limits . . . but these are still in full growth."

And he concludes by establishing a contrast doubtless more impressive today than when it was written:

The American struggles against natural obstacles; the adversaries of the Russian are men; the former combats the wilderness and savage life; the latter, civilization with all its weapons and its arts; the conquests of the one are mighty through the plow; those of the other through the sword. To attain his goal the American relies on personal interest, and gives free rein to the untrammeled efforts and common sense of the citizens; the Russian concentrates all the authority of society in a single arm: the principal instrument of the one is freedom, of the other slavery. The points of departure are different as are also the routes. And, nevertheless, both seem marked by the will of Heaven to control the destinies of half a planet.

And foreseeing also that the ideal of liberty and progress pursued by man would one day be a reality, as indeed it is today in large measure, the author of *Democracy in America* prophesied with equal discernment the dilemma in which we now find ourselves: "The nations of our time cannot prevent men from attaining freedom, despite their unequal conditions; but it will depend on men themselves whether the principle of liberty is to make them slave or free; whether it is to lead them to understanding and knowledge or to barbarism; to prosperity or to ruin." No more precise words have been written in our day about the blind alley to which humanity has arrived, one that brings about a recrudescence of the Europe-America debate to which we have alluded.

One of the most recent and significant manifestations is seen in the discussion between Arnold Toynbee and Max Lerner on the occasion of the NATO (North Atlantic Treaty Organization) meeting in December of 1958. It is reproduced by the review *Occident*.[3]

The question was posited around the hypothesis that a new type of civilization has arisen in the United States, one capable of replacing that of Europe as a directing force. Lerner begins by acknowledging the debt of the United States to Europe and reproves equally those Americans who would forget their past and the Europeans who fancy themselves the sole legatees of the spirit and traditions of the West. He believes, however, that "the Americans have created something unique, something neither a reflection nor a corruption of European culture. . . . America has become the archtype of a new thought and feeling, the only hope of our epoch." Opposing that archtype he sees only one other of identical power and capacity for attraction: the Russian.

This is the same thesis that Lerner had already expounded in an important book, *America as a Civilization*. His arguments in the debate with Toynbee are not always convincing. None of the factors or facts that he adduces is, strictly speaking, new or peculiar to the United States. Such is the case with industrialization and democracy. To this, however, he replies that there are fundamental differences of degree and method in their operation. From these differences springs what he calls a new "structure of technology and force" or "a different system of energy and will," the basis of an original civilization, the North American, moving toward the creation of a new humanism. Lerner sees further proof of this in the visible process of the Americanization of Europe.

We should recall in passing how, as we have indicated before,* Jacques Maritain sees in the United States the possibility of a future humanism. But the French philosopher suggests as possible what Lerner considers already achieved.

Toynbee, disagreeing with Lerner's theories, maintains the essential identity of Europeans and Americans. "The latter," he affirms, "have not been able to escape their condition as men and sinners, the condition, in short, of all the citizens of the Western World. The United States has created neither a new language nor a new religion, necessary attributes if one is to speak of a new civilization. . . . Everything induces me to conclude," he says by way of summation, "that the

* See pp. 74–75.

United States is a part of a larger community, the community of Western peoples. That is not all: the Western community is in the process of joining a universal society that will eventually include all the human race, provided humanity does not commit autogenocide before that time."

In the final analysis Toynbee agrees with Ortega y Gasset, another European voice, when the latter denies that the United States possesses historical maturity: "No; it is not yet possible to define the American, for the simple reason that he does not yet exist; as yet he has not irrevocably wagered his existence, has not committed himself to being a specific type of man. As yet he has not begun his history." [4]

Let us cite another piece of testimony, more considered and perhaps more exact, that of Alfonso Reyes, given during a colloquy on cultural relations between Europe and Latin America. He says: "To speak of Latin American civilization in the present connection would be inopportune: this would lead us to the area of archeology, alien to our subject. To speak of Latin American culture would be somewhat equivocal: that would make us think only of a branch of the European tree transplanted to American soil. On the other hand we can speak properly of Latin American intelligence, its vision of life, and its participation therein. This will permit us to define, although provisionally, the tone of America." [5]

Ortega y Gasset spoke in 1932, Reyes in 1936. It is not difficult to perceive that since that time something has changed the slightly defensive tone of Toynbee and the somewhat petulant assurance of Lerner. But we are not concerned now with solving this thorny problem. If we have called attention to it, it is because we consider it a pertinent introduction to another subject: the confrontation of the two most important cultures of this Continent.

II

AT the outset let us note that today the Europe-America debate is almost exclusively between the United States and Europe. Spanish- and Portuguese-speaking America is absent from it and rarely mentioned, as though it counted for nothing in deciding the destiny of Western man and of man in general. This is a phenomenon paralleling the lack of interest, apparent during the last twenty years, of the United States in their former good neighbors to the south; on a larger scale it corresponds to the decline that the countries of Latin, Catholic, and Mediterranean Europe have suffered in general world organizations. This is a deterioration that France herself has barely managed to escape only because of her prestige.

If we wish to arrive at a complete understanding of our problem, we should start from one basic, ineludible fact: the systematic scorn for the Hispanic cultures and Hispanic man in the modern world. That such disdain may have its explanation within the body of values in force during the last few centuries neither invalidates its existence nor justifies its excesses and injustices in many cases. This is a scorn, moreover, probably not unconnected with the almost sickly penchant for pessimistic self-dissection to which Spaniards on both sides of the Atlantic Ocean have been addicted for some time; nor is it unrelated, we may add, to the deep-rooted dissentions that divide them.

But, even so, never have there been more evident indications that Hispanic, Latin, Iberian, or Indo-Hispanic America—the name here is the least important element—after more than a century of painful ascent and turbulence, is making ready, amidst the agitations that today are disturbing her, to enact the role assigned her by history, tradition, her geographical vastness, and even her very complexity.

There has been, of course, both in the United States and in the other Western countries, the tacit or explicit, and at times involuntary, recognition of the fact that the Hispanic world possesses perhaps supreme values in its way of understanding life and facing reality. But ordinarily these same values are exalted rhetorically in inter-American gatherings, be these academic or political, while as a matter of fact they are scorned in the field of action.

Subsequently we shall see how important changes have been taking place in the United States, not only in the understanding of Hispanic-American culture but also in the interest and regard for it as well. For example, no one can deny the flourishing state and growth of Hispanic studies during the last forty years. Nevertheless, from the outset it is important to stress the negative factors so that later we may be in a position to appreciate better the obvious changes in the historical perspective.

Let us, then, enumerate certain of these negative factors:

1. In cultural and university centers the always doubtful prestige of the Hispanic disciplines does not stand in equitable relation either to their values, significance, and importance or to the increase in Hispanic studies to which we have alluded.

2. One cannot overlook the ignorance or semi-ignorance of the average North American about the other countries of the Continent. With the exception of Canada, they are for him little more than backward and underdeveloped nations and, at best, picturesque, rich in revolutions and dance music. As a matter of fact it is usually only of Mexico and the Caribbean that he has even the remotest idea.

3. Politically and economically speaking, since the days of the "Good Neighbor Policy," the right has been assumed to dictate the destiny of these nations, as with one's own property, either trying to win their consent or forcing their acquiescence if circumstances so dictate. In this area, as in many others, there are already numerous signs of fundamental change. This fact notwithstanding, it can be said that even today, when the still very recent triumphs of the liberal and democratic spirit in the majority of the Hispanic-American countries point to definitive and transcendental changes, the average American and, sad though it may be to say it, many others view the least sign of social transformation with irrepressible alarm.

All of this stems from long ago and has very deep roots. The feeling of Anglo-Saxon superiority in relationships with other peoples, along with the conviction that only their countries possess the secret of free and democratic living, is inherent in the American, as it has been in the Englishman.

This affirmation is, of course, overly simplified and exaggerated. As for the United States, such an assertion takes into account neither the existence of an equalitarian sentiment consubstantial with the American ideal nor the fact that the Nordic man of the United States has, during the last hundred years, absorbed in his veins more blood from different European to say nothing of Asiatic and African, countries than has been the case with any other nation in the world. Naturally I am not speaking in strictly biological or ethnical terms. The phenomenon is above all historical and social. But one must not forget that the torrent of immigration alters essentially neither mental structure, nor the three or four basic principles on which the American has built what Américo Castro has called his vital "dwelling-place" [6] or abode, his manner of living and being. The emigrant is immediately absorbed—as is the case in many of our countries—and only on the margins, on what we could call the fringes of social incorporation, do we find a restless and unassimilated minority. On some levels we find the gangster, the racketeer, the Mafia, so much a subject of discussion now in the United States; at a higher level, because it borders on the world of ideas, we have the "radical" artist, intellectual, or politician—years ago an anarchist, today perhaps a fellow traveler—ordinarily of Jewish, Slavic, or Italian name. After these reservations, and returning to the typical attitude of the American, it is not an exaggeration to assert that for him nothing is farther removed from the possibility of a true democracy than the America of Indo-Iberian origin.

Only if one keeps in mind the deep historical roots of the fundamental differences between the Americas is it possible to comprehend the phenomenon, to understand the inveterate nature of those convictions or simple prejudices. We have seen, in the foregoing part of this study, what the fundamental attitudes of the United States toward Spain have been throughout history, attitudes born of an old and deep-seated cultural rivalry, as was so clearly recognized by F. E. Chadwick in his study of the origins of the Spanish-American War.

And that rivalry continues in various forms during the century and a half of independence of the Ibero-American countries. Nevertheless, it is not uncommon that so significant a fact is either not always perceived or not admitted with due clarity, not so much by people seeking a certain immediate end as by those who would understand historical processes. They confront complex problems as though America had no history: the North Americans through a desire to deny it, or to obscure it in a majority of cases; the Hispanic-Americans through a lack of solidarity with the Spanish past. At times it comes from ignorance, at others from haste, at still others from a simple desire for change. Whether the Spanish past be glorious or heinous cannot be elucidated now. But if we have learned anything from the modern study of historical processes, it is that in private life, as in the workings of history, we are the product of what has happened to us. Furthermore, we can cease to be this to any appreciable degree only through the understanding of our surroundings, in order to plan, in the terms of Ortega y Gasset, our job, our life project. It is only on the basis of a previous consciousness of whence we came that we can, with any degree of efficiency, plan our desired destination.

There are a number of authors—among them Eduardo Caballero Calderón and Leopoldo Zea—who in recent years have raised this question of the two Americas and their antecedents with remarkable clarity and perspicacity. However, because of its greater concision, I would rather refer to an article by Luis Araquistain entitled "La disputa entre Europa y América," which appeared in the review *La Torre*. It was written on the occasion of the Rencontres Internationales de Genève of 1954, where the subject was debated again, and here Araquistain analyzes the prolongation in the New World of discrepancies existing among the great European cultures.

Let us examine how he focuses the question. Although my quotation is rather lengthy, I am including only those parts germane to our purpose and omitting almost completely the interesting résumé of the characteristics of various cultures. His point of departure is the idea that it is wrong to speak simply of Europe and America. He continues:

There is more than one Europe and more than one America. There are at least three Europes: Nordic or Anglo-Germanic; Southern, Latin, or Mediterranean; Oriental or Slavic. Let us leave the last-named out of account . . . Nordic and Southern Europe remain.

There are similarly three Americas on the American continent: North or Anglo-Saxon America (the United States and Canada), a historical and cultural prolongation of Anglo-Germanic Europe . . . ; Hispanic or Latin America, a historical and cultural extension of Latin or Mediterranean Europe; and indigenous America. In the interest of simplification let us also eliminate this aboriginal America from consideration, an America which until now has been little more than a passive historical reality.

There are no essential differences between the two Americas and the two Europes, viewed in their respective cultural parallels. There are doubtless quantitative, but certainly not qualitative, differences. In Anglo-Saxon America we find characteristics very similar to those of Anglo-Germanic Europe.

The characteristics of Latin America are similar to those of European countries of related culture. . . .

Before proffering a judgment on so vast a question, i.e., whether America is superior to Europe or vice versa . . . , it would be fruitful to ponder the differences between the two Europes and the two Americas,—between Southern-Mediterranean and Nordic or Anglo-Germanic Europe; between North or Anglo-Saxon and Hispanic America. What are the reasons for such diversity? Is it a question of racial, anthropological causes, and as such not reducible to a common type of civilization? Is there a Mediterranean or Latin race in Europe and America capable of being organized into democratic, stable, and efficient states; states based on an ordered, creative, and vigorous economy, like the English or North American, like those of the Low Countries, the Scandinavian and, we hope, like the new German state? Is there perhaps an inherent technical, economic, and political incapacity in the peoples of Greco-Roman culture of both continents?

Did the Catholic religion have an influence in the decadence of those states in its check of the capitalistic spirit of the budding bourgeoisie, whereas Protestantism spurred it on in the Nordic states?

And Araquistain answers these questions:

Certainly there are many reasons for this differentiation between the two Europes, afterwards to be projected in the two Americas: some of them political (Caesarian ambition for a universal empire, first seen in the Spanish monarchs of the House of Austria, later in Louis XIV of France and in Napoleon); others economic (the mercantilist error); others geographical (the discovery of America, displacing the center of European civilization from the Mediterranean to the Atlantic); still others in the areas of education and cultural life (the seignorial or bourgeois concept of life, Catholic or Protestant preparation for this or the other life). But the fact is there and it is as useless to try to deny it as to try to demonstrate it. What today is understood as American superiority and Americanism or Americanization, in another period went by the name of Britannic superiority or Anglicization.[7]

The view of the problem by Caballero Calderón in his valuable book *Americanos y europeos* is similar in point of departure to that of Araquistain. "Just as Europe," he says, "breaks apart geographically and historically into two Europes that draw farther and farther from one another, so in the New World there are two Americas clearly differentiated by history and geography." He then points to the existence of an American common denominator in relations with the Old World: "As for Americans, they all present a solid psychological bloc vis-à-vis Europeans. As for Anglo-Saxons and Ibero-Americans, there are profound differences between them."[8]

Zea, who has been studying this subject diligently for some time, presents the problem in even more trenchant terms when, in his latest book *América en la historia*, he emphasizes the basic divergencies between the Iberian and the Occidental as these exist in the modern world. According to him, Anglo-Saxon America not only assimilates the spirit of Western culture but also exemplifies its natural and maximum development. On the other hand, Hispanic America is born of a culture that had opposed the normal course of the West, and had been defeated in its opposition. "The triumph of the modern spirit in Europe," he says, "had also meant the defeat of Spain, which had opposed it. Spain, and with Spain, Portugal and the Latin world had been placed outside the new expression of culture, the so-called occidental culture; that is to say, outside history." [9]

Elsewhere, in *Ensayos sobre filosofía en la historia*, Zea had, years before, spoken of the feeling of security of the American, based on his great material development, and of the dual sense of inferiority of the Hispanic American "vis-à-vis Europe and its culture" on the one hand, and "vis-à-vis the practical spirit of the United States on the other." [10]

Adducing these opinions does not imply their total acceptance on our part. The phenomenon we are considering is extremely complex, and it is scarcely necessary to point out how every affirmation like those above gives rise to inevitable differentiations and clarifications. Our only purpose is to call attention to certain ideas of responsible writers, worth keeping in mind as we study our subject.

Naturally, when one categorically proclaims British or, in our time, American superiority, one is speaking, as is the case with the authors we have cited, in purely relative terms. They are referring to fundamentally political and economic values that have ruled modern societies since the industrial and democratic revolutions, not to absolute and permanent ones. There are, moreover, reasons to believe that today we are witnessing the transvaluation or, if you will, the dissolution of those values through the eruption of powerful forces.

The most important of such forces might be said to be the movement of the third Europe to the foreground of the historical stage—the Oriental and Slavic Europe which Araquistain disregarded in his scheme to facilitate the parallel. Perhaps also the third America, the indigenous or aboriginal, is likewise preparing to play a full historical role.

Independently of this, one must consider the existence of factors inherent to the essential meaning of America that from the beginning have pointed to unity, to continental compenetration. We might mention, among others, the geographic, the psychological-social and the historico-demographic.

There is no doubt that despite geographical differences, and with difficulties of communication and the resultant isolation of many sections now overcome, the unity and continuity of the Continent is an undeniable fact. And psychologically, the people who at various times inhabited the new lands—conqueror, settler, or pioneer—shared a common orientation toward the future, a search for new goals, realities and ideals, aims ever renewed by the waves of immigration.

Historically the European cultures have been mixed and modified on contact with native cultures or simply with virgin lands. Thus crossbreeding has arisen, more pronounced in the Hispanic portion of America but not totally absent in the North. The latter is the case because, although there was only a very limited mixing with the aboriginal races, one can assume the absorption of a certain telluric effluvium, as Keyserling thought, or even of the ancestral spirit of the Indian. Moreover, the great mixture of bloods from many different peoples, in the colossal melting pot of the last hundred years, has somehow given rise to a phenomenon, if not identical, at least analogus in nature to what has occurred in Hispanic America.

It is from the complexity of factors we have been discussing that there arises the extremely complicated interplay, fascinating at times for an attentive observer, of clashes and attractions, of conflicts and harmonies characteristic of the history of the two Americas.

III

WE should now see how these two great human blocs have fared in their trying propinquity, how amidst mutual inhibitions, clashes, and misunderstandings—to say nothing of abuses and injustices—there has been taking form the still cloudy, but nevertheless real, consciousness of a substantially common destiny. And, finally, we should examine how the future is being projected in an insecure present, replete with uncertainties and disagreement.

Cultural questions interest us particularly: general values, attitudes, ideas, creation. Although one should not overlook the importance of political and economic factors, Alfonso Reyes was right when, in the lecture to which we have alluded before,* he proclaimed the pre-eminence of intellectual values: "Such communication between intellectuals will necessarily produce political effects. It would be childish to overlook this eventuality. And all should realize that political participation is a general attribute shared by all men. Politics is not a posted preserve. Every human act is reflected in the *polis* and everything redounds in good or evil from mens' living together. When the intellectuals of America have shaken hands, American political life will have changed fundamentally."

* See p. 84.

One is forced to recognize that Reyes' ideal, that hand-clasp by the intellectuals of both continents, is still far from a reality. And this is surely not the fault of those who write in Spanish and Portuguese. Many, and among them the best, have made repeated efforts to understand the brother or the enemy of the north. Some, like Sarmiento, have surrendered almost completely. As we shall see, there have been gestures of reciprocity. But basically, neither has the Hispanic American been disposed, ever (let it be said in his honor), to abdicate his own being and adopt what for him have been very doubtful values; nor has the North American, except on the rarest occasions, wished to renounce his consubstantial, and of course false, sense of superiority.

No sooner does the Anglo-American become conscious of his historical reality and of his future in Colonial New England, than one can detect in him an interest, albeit still vague, in the rest of the hemisphere. And it is not difficult to discern in him certain characteristics which, with the inevitable variations of each passing moment, will take on a permanent character: the expansionist aim and evangelizing proselytism. With time the first will become the idea of Manifest Destiny of Jefferson, and this in turn will become the Monroe Doctrine. As for evangelizing proselytism, this will take the form of extending to the lands of the south the benefits of Protestantism, the true religion, later to be equated with the benefits of modernity, of true Western civilization. The amalgamation of the religious and the temporal in Puritan ideology, as a basis of the American state and of its expansionist spirit, has already been thoroughly studied by Ralph Barton Perry, Herbert Schneider, and Vernon Louis Parrington. Among Spanish-speaking authors it has been investigated by Angélica Mendoza in her book *Fuentes del pensamiento de los Estados Unidos,* where there is a precise résumé of the particular aspect that concerns us. She says: "This theocracy justified itself by affirming that it was a 'democracy' of the 'chosen' whose obvious destiny was the restoration of God in the virgin lands of America. Both the Calvinist doctrine of the state, supported by its leaders, as well as the personal certainty of each Puritan that he was in possession of irresistible 'grace' . . . gave it a missionary content and a comfortable security for any kind of enterprises the theocracy might undertake . . . since it felt itself to be the instrument of divine decisions." [11]

This explains the zeal of the Puritans Cotton Mather and Samuel Sewall about which we have spoken earlier.* Perhaps what is not seen so clearly is the persistence of this attitude and of the same principles during more than two centuries: the missionary inspiration, for example, behind the Good Neighbor Policy when, from Washington, D.C., Franklin D. Roosevelt, Cordell Hull, and Adolf Berle spoke of the need to fortify the political independence and territorial integrity of the nations of the New World through an increase in their economic well-being, with the purpose of "promoting a general advance in civilization."

An identical consciousness of their role as a chosen people—a feeling, moreover, much repeated in history—is reflected by many American decisions: when Woodrow Wilson decided to enter the First World War in order to make the world safe for democracy, or when Roosevelt, in the Atlantic Charter, proclaimed the Four Freedoms, when the Point Four Program was enacted and, in general, when Americans assign themselves the mission of saving from tyranny, political instability, ignorance, sickness, or poverty those peoples they consider underdeveloped. *Mutatis mutandis,* the justification of English colonialism was no different.

It would be an oversimplification to believe—although such is frequently the case—that this attitude is attributable

* See pp. 19–20.

simply to plans for domination or exploitation or that it is a hypocritical mantle covering purely political designs. To think thus is to ignore the distance that historically separates realities and ideologies; it is to ignore the fact that the material and the spiritual, deed and idea, self-interest and idealistic impulse are ever intermingled in the actions of men and peoples.

When the United States is accused of materialism one must not forget, if indeed such an accusation is entirely just, that this is the product of a historical and mental structure, of a way of understanding life that is ideological and even spiritual in origin. All of which by no means invalidates the reservations or even the accusations that have so often been made about their inter-American policy.

Leopoldo Zea makes a fair appraisal of the problem:

> It is not a question of a lack of understanding of American civilization; neither would we begrudge the people of the United States recognition for their great collaboration in Western culture. No, the facts are that the values and the banners which the Americans hoist, such as liberty, sovereignty, and national happiness, are not compatible with the attitudes their country adopts in relation to the peoples who yearn to attain them; vis-à-vis peoples who endeavor to follow their example. American democracy is not compatible with the aid and comfort that the United States gives to tyrannies in Latin America to defend the interests of its companies and trusts that have invested there.[12]

These are very just words of which almost all the liberal spirits of the United States would, and do, approve. Moreover, Samuel Flagg Bemis (a historian certainly not to be suspected of excessive liberalism), despite his wishing to justify many scarcely justifiable policies and actions in his book, *The Latin America Policy of the United States*, recognizes without hesitation that the missionary endeavor to which we have alluded "has not served to curb imperialism or political intervention; on the contrary." [13]

At the heart of the matter—as is the case in all great historical conflicts—is the deep-rooted nature of certain convictions, in part well-founded and in part erroneous. It is not that the United States proclaims the superiority of its civilization simply to justify a policy in many instances abusive; on the contrary, they really believe in it and in the legitimacy of their motives when, for example, they defend the investments of their capitalists.

In the *America Hispana* of Waldo Frank there is a three-page vignette of the American businessman that should give us cause for meditation:

First to be noted, is that he acts in good faith. To regard him as a villain malignantly plotting the destruction of peoples is to underestimate his menace. He is dangerous, because he believes fanatically in himself and in his good intentions. He does not doubt that his work in the one-sided development of the resources of Latin America, and in the spreading of American products and American standards, is the salvation of inferior peoples. This service he assumes to be so great that any means to it is justified. He deplores the occasional need of force or interference in local matters: but he is the carrier of a dominant ideal, Progress.[14]

In the light of this conviction, which naturally is not that of all the United States, but to be sure that of a very representative sector, the Hispanic American doubtless believes, with equal justification, in the superiority of the moral and human values embodied in his own civilization. And, moreover, apart from other quarrels born of abuse and insult, he cannot accept seeing himself treated as a second-class citizen of a second-class people.

From this disparity of convictions is born the pejorative and oversimplified view: the cliché. The United States, the country of the dollar, is many things. It has thousands of schools, colleges, universities, and libraries which support a rich cultural and scientific life. It is a nation of philanthropists; it has produced great statesmen such as Jefferson and Lincoln. Its philosophers and thinkers include men like Emerson, James, Royce, or Dewey. Its extraordinary literature numbers among its distinguished figures Poe, Whitman, Mark Twain, Melville, and Henry James or, in our time, Frost, Sandburg, Sinclair Lewis, O'Neill, Eliot, Faulkner, Hemingway and many others. Such is not the land of noisy and uncouth exploiters that at times both Europeans and Hispanic Americans delight in scorning; nor is Hispanic America, justly proud of its traditions, of its great cities, and its culture which, discounting the pre-Columbian civilizations, antedates that of the United States by two centuries, the chaotic, backward, ungovernable, and indolent world that its neighbors imagine.

IV

THE truth is that from the beginning of Hispanic America's role in history, from the period of the precursors and fathers of its independence, the currents of understanding and even the feeling of unity have been equally genuine and powerful. And so Nariño, Miranda, Mejía, or Mariano Moreno and Belgrano saw in the independence of the great northern republic a model and a guide. The revolutionary agents of the period of the uprising found in the new state welcome, encouragement, and at times aid in their struggle with Spain, despite the fact that the United States government was hamstrung by the touchy negotiations on Florida. Henry Clay obtained, not without overcoming resistance and caution, recognition for the different nations as they successfully broke away from the mother country. And when the Monroe Doctrine was proclaimed in 1823 it was generally well received on the greater part of the Continent.

From the beginning, however, there were warning voices. Diego Portales wrote in 1822: "The President of the North American Federation has said: 'it is recognized that America is for Americans.' Be careful not to escape one domination only to fall into another. . . . I believe that all of this conforms to a prearranged plan going somewhat as follows: effect the conquest of America, not by force, but through *in-*

fluence in every sphere. This will happen, perhaps not today but surely tomorrow."

In the same year Bolívar wrote to Santander: "Later I find in the lead . . . a powerful nation, rich, warlike, and capable of everything. This nation is the enemy of Europe and presently is opposing the powerful English; it is a country that in turn will wish to dictate the law to us and will do so irremissibly." And years later he wrote to Estanislao Vergara: "The United States, so fond of their own freedom, do not show the same concern about the liberties of others. Quite the contrary, they have converted that very liberty into an instrument for bringing misery to other peoples." [15]

It is to be noted that the United States refused various proposals for alliance—with Chile (1824), with Colombia (1824), and with Brazil (1825)—as well as the promise of aid which Mexico asked for in 1825 and Río de la Plata in 1826. And, finally, it did not participate in the Panama Congress called by Bolívar, and thus contributed to its failure. The watchword of President John Quincy Adams was that of "contracting no alliances and avoiding entanglements."

This marks the beginning of a long history that need not be recalled to the Hispanic-American reader. Generally speaking, during the nineteenth century the Monroe Doctrine did not prevent various attacks by Spain, England, or France on different parts of the Continent; nor did continental solidarity stay acts of aggression by the United States, the most serious of which was the one that wrested from Mexico a considerable part of what was once her territory. Neither did it prevent vacillation with respect to aid for the Cubans in their long struggle with the mother country, although Cuban independence and even the desire to incorporate that country into its system had been deeply rooted in the minds of Washington administrations from the beginning.

But it is in the field of cultural relations—which interest us particularly—where one can best see the forces operating in the evolution of the Hispanic-American peoples during the nineteenth century. There seem to be three dominant currents: the first—moving since the ideological beginnings of Latin-American independence—is pointed toward Europe and more specifically toward France, and we can call it, although the term is excessive, Gallicization; another would be aversion to Spain, which in some cases becomes a declared hatred of the mother country. The third is the contradictory attitude toward the United States: a mixture of admiration and caution, a desire for imitation and understanding on the one hand, and on the other distrust and an awareness of differences. A rigorous discussion of this matter would demand shadings and certain necessary qualifications. Our purpose would be to show how, for example, along with the French influences of Romanticism and Positivism, there were other important ones of varied origin, principally English—Bentham, Reid, Hamilton, John Stuart and James Mill or, in the literary sphere, Byron, Scott, Ossian, Shelley, Tennyson, etc.—and, in lesser degree, German or Italian.

As for hatred of Spain, when one applies rigorous historical objectivity to a study of the relations of the Hispanic-American literatures with that of Spain, it will be found that not all thought, as did Sarmiento, Lastarria, or Bilbao that "to civilize is to de-Hispanize"; that apart from defenders of the Hispanic tradition as little suspect as Bello, the greater or lesser influence of Spanish writers is never wanting at any moment: from Feijóo, Jovellanos, or Meléndez in the eighteenth century, to Galdós, Bécquer or even Campoamor and Núñez de Arce, passing through pre-Romantics or Romantics like Quintana, Larra, Zorrilla, or Espronceda. Recall, also, the collaboration of émigrés like Blanco White, Alcalá

Galiano, and José Joaquín de Mora with their Hispanic-American companions in London, or Rubén Darío devouring the volumes of the Rivadeneira publishing house in the Biblioteca Nacional of Nicaragua.

Although this is not our subject, it would not be alien to its complete understanding to recall, along with the conflict and attraction of the two Americas, the everpresent consciousness of European and Spanish tradition and the fact that the assimilation and mixture of various influences is one of the outstanding traits of Ibero-American culture.

With regard to the United States, it is obvious that there is scarcely a Hispanic-American writer, politician, or thinker who has not in one period or another, at times with enthusiasm, at others with distrust, and occasionally even with manifest hostility, drawn near to the culture of his Anglo-Saxon neighbors or come to grips with this problem of the two Americas. Ordinarily people look to the United States as a desirable model because of its technical and political accomplishments—democracy, progress, unity. The bibliography on the subject is copious and from this I recommend, especially because of its well-integrated résumé, the previously cited doctoral dissertation of José de Onís, *The United States as Seen by Spanish American Writers, 1776–1890*. In this work the ideas and attitudes of the most representative men, from Bolívar, Miranda, Simón Rodríguez, Fray Servando Teresa de Mier, Rocafuerte, or Heredia to Alberdi, Lastarria, Bilbao, Alamán, Montalvo, Vicuña Mackenna or Sarmiento, are clearly summarized.

As Onís observes, it is Sarmiento—otherwise so profoundly Hispanic—who represents the high point in the positive evaluation of the United States as a model worthy of emulation. In this connection we would call attention to the final words of his book *Conflictos y armonías de las razas en América:* "South America is falling behind and will lose its providential mission as a branch of modern civilization. Let us not detain the United States in its march—the long-range aim of certain people. Let us catch up with the United States. Let us be America as the sea shares the nature of the ocean. Let us be United States."

Soon there were going to be reasons to distrust such enthusiasm, changes of direction and spirit. Before examining them, let us point to two facts: the limited influence of the United States in the strictly literary sphere and their almost total indifference toward the culture of their neighbors, a thing that contrasts with the interest in the romantic image of the Spanish past that we examined earlier. With the exception of Fenimore Cooper and Longfellow, North American literature does not have in Hispanic America an echo parallel and comparable to the overall interest in the United States, its institutions, and its new type of man. When the influence of Emerson, Poe, or Whitman begins, we are on the threshold of another period which in the political area will be one of maximum tension.

As we have noted, the attitude of the United States, if we discount the interest of its historians, headed by Prescott, is one of obvious indifference. Bemis has recognized this fact with laudable frankness and says that "after the earlier interests of the Era of Emancipation had subsided, one regrets to say that there developed a general indifference toward Latin American culture, if not actual contempt for it. . . . The region and its peoples remained to the northern republic a profitable place to trade with, an interesting field for explorers and geographers, a continent of opportunity for pioneer engineers, a romantic land for footloose soldiers of fortune, a vast and challenging field for Protestant missionary competition." [16]

This attitude is going to become even more pronounced as a result of profound changes in American society following the defeat of the southern states in the Civil War, states characterized by an almost exclusively agrarian spirit. With industrial development at its height in the North, capitalism enters its ascendency, and we have the period of the new "robber barons," of the "great mogols" with their characteristic aggressiveness, egotism, and insolence. This is the so-called Gilded Age, studied critically by, among others, Charles A. and Mary R. Beard in *The Rise of American Civilization;* and in *The Education of Henry Adams* the crisis in moral values during this period, one aspect of which was a marked anti-intellectualism, is treated in some of the most profound pages in all North American literature. These are the moments when José Martí—the Hispanic American who best understood the United States, and the one who judged them most serenely—wrote his well-known and significant lines: "We love the country of Lincoln, but we fear the country of Cutting."

At the end of the century two factors contributed to an unleashing of expansionist appetites: the victory over Spain, which converted the United States into an international power in the two great oceans; and a change in the age-old balance of power with the ascendency of Japan in the Pacific and Germany in the world of the Atlantic. From this sprang American imperialism, big-stick and dollar diplomacy, interventions, and the protection of the country's investors.

Certain historians of the United States, without denying the facts, attempt to justify them by stressing their transitory and moderate character, and even their intent to guarantee the security of the American peoples. This prevented neither obvious abuses—Mexico, Panama, Santo Domingo, Nicaragua—nor general alarm in the whole of Hispanic America. All the intellectuals, from the young student groups to the greatest writers, exalted in prose and verse the ideal of political, spiritual, or simply human independence; meanwhile the chancelleries weathered the storm, and disquieting revolutionary threats arose here and there in protest against the odious combination of local dictators and what was viewed, rightly or wrongly, as the Yankee exploiter.

I would cite the opinions of two individuals who judged the spiritual state of the youth during those years. Neither is marked by its partisanship nor by its exaggeratedly patriotic or revolutionary turbulence. One is by Roberto F. Giusti in his beautiful essay "Una generación juvenil de comienzos de siglo":

> People feared the United States, which some publicists and propagandists liked to represent as voracious Caliban, opposing poor little Ariel, the pitiful little republics of Hispanic America. I don't recall whether Manuel Ugarte had already begun his publicist's campaign against the "Yankee Colossus," but that opposition was present in everyone's mind. . . . The *Cantos de vida y esperanza* of Rubén Darío are of 1905, in which we read enthusiastically the magnificent apostrophe to Theodore Roosevelt. . . .
> If we opened the *Viaje intelectual* of Groussac, published in 1904 . . . we found the lecture delivered six years before in the Victoria Theatre during the war between Spain and the United States, a diatribe against the northern republic. . . . If we read the *Ariel* of Rodó, the anthem was the same, although the tone was different.[17]

In a page of *El estudiante de la mesa redonda,* Germán Arciniegas, years later, notes more pointedly the corrupting effects of commercial penetration by the United States: "The government wished to borrow money. The agents of the United States banks pressured the defenseless states into asking them for loans. The sons of the presidents and government ministers were bribed. Big deals were arranged, automobiles were given as presents, and the morality of the poor nations was prostituted."[18]

Giusti is speaking of Argentina at the beginning of the

century; Arciniegas, a Colombian, describes the situation in the year 1918. Testimony from other countries or other writers would amply confirm their views. This is the period of greatest misunderstanding, abuses, and suspicions between two worlds which represent the two cultures whose relations we have been reviewing.

This anti-imperialistic and anti-Yankee feeling of the first decades of the present century coincides with, and in a measure determines, certain currents and happenings of major significance in the contemporary evolution of the Hispanic-American peoples. Among these could be mentioned a new rapprochement with Europe—the devotion of the Modernists to France, a feeling for the great Greco-Roman tradition exalted by Rodó, an incipient cult of the art of Renaissance Italy, and, a little later, an awakening of interest in German philosophy. At the same time there is evidence of a new consciousness of the common Hispanic past, a current of friendliness toward Spain. Rather than of the mother country (the subject of official and academic discourses), people think of the common language, of moral and spiritual values saved from ruin and decadence, of the blood of *Hispania fecunda*. Or they think of the infant and renascent Spain invoked by Rodó, a Spain which one day may join the swelling march, not of her daughters, but of her sisters, once Spaniards and Hispanic Americans have freed themselves of the evils of an obscurantist past. Unamuno, Ortega y Gasset, Azorín, Machado, Juan Ramón Jiménez, Valle-Inclán or, later, García Lorca, are acclaimed as masters. This is the spirit of brotherhood that saw its most glorious moment when thousands of Hispanic Americans participated in the triumph and defense of the Second Spanish Republic as though it were something very much their own.

In another area—pursuing our examination of currents and

phenomena during the first thirty years of the century—we see the growth of an international feeling, allied theoretically with socialism, and even with communism, still romantically conceived during the twenties. This feeling stood in paradoxical union with the high tide of nationalistic movements and the assertion of a belief in the similarity of problems and destinies of all Spanish- and Portuguese-speaking peoples of the Continent.

Another important factor is the concern for the indigenous populations and their problems, either as a source of literary inspiration or as an imperative for the necessary redemption of the Indian, the victim of so many historical forces.

All of this coincides with two developments destined to have deep future repercussions: the Mexican Revolution (the first social revolution in America) and the youth movement for university reform. The latter will have mentors like Ingenieros and Vasconcelos and, in the long run, will reveal the strong desire for a deep-running educational program reaching all strata of society.

Within such a framework, divorce from the culture of the United States, or a lack of interest in it, is stimulated by the optimistic and noble, but nonetheless deceptive, oversimplifications of Rodó, Rubén Darío, and many others, who say in effect that, opposed to North American imperialism, the kingdom of Caliban, Latin America—our America—is the only repository of spiritual values in the New World.

The result of all this was that until the years of the Good Neighbor Policy, with the arrival of Waldo Frank and his noble mission of brotherhood, it was possible, as Luis Alberto Sánchez shows in a chapter of his book *Un sudamericano en Norteamérica*,[19] for people in Hispanic America to believe that the United States, a land that has won six Nobel Prizes so far in this century, was a country without literature and spirit.

V

EVERYONE is familiar with recent history. The somewhat idylic era of the Good Neighbor Policy, whose seeds fortunately have not entirely withered, although at times it would seem so, was followed by the last postwar period in which American policy has provoked so much well-founded distrust. It is only fair to recognize that the statesmen of Washington have been compelled to improvise, incessantly harassed by pressures from the four corners of the globe, in order to assume a world leadership for which, perhaps, in view of the short historical role of the country, they were not prepared. This fact can attenuate, but never entirely justify, the seriousness of certain errors: lack of interest in the countries of the Continent and indifference toward the economic crises suffered by many; connivance with antidemocratic governments whose compliance in the so-called Cold War is taken for granted; and, in consonance with this, the support of bloody dictatorships, tolerating, if not promoting, the situation described in all its details by Germán Arciniegas in his book *Entre la libertad y el miedo*.

Today, following the strong upsurge of liberal and democratic forces in all of Hispanic America, and after certain incidents that it is unnecessary to recall, there are unquestionable signs of a radical change. Hispanic-American affairs are again of current importance, and, notwithstanding the repeated crises of the last few months—Berlin, the Middle East, China—scarcely a day passes when, either through official channels in Washington or in the most responsible segments of the press, Latin-American problems are not debated. There is no doubt that, as a recent headline of the New York *Times* indicates, "Latin American Relations Take on a New Look." Manifestations of that new look could be said to be, among other things, the various meetings of the twenty-one nations and, more specifically, the Buenos Aires meeting, where a solution was sought to certain pressing economic problems; President Eisenhower's proposal to Congress that it appropriate $450,000,000 as the contribution of the United States to the Inter-American Bank; the new attitude regarding the establishment of the Common Market and concerning the stabilization of production and prices of certain products; the already implemented economic and technical aid to Bolivia; the new report of the Subcommittee on American Republics Affairs on aid and reconsideration of policies governing armament shipments; and even that somewhat naïve motto of "the cold shoulder to the dictators and a new cordiality toward democratic governments." [20]

To be sure, Washington has proceeded under unfavorable pressures and in response to alarming warnings, such as those sounded by Muñoz Marín in an article in *Look* entitled "It is Later Than We Think in Latin America," or the more recent ones of former President Figueres of Costa Rica on the force of the "anti-Yankee and anti-Western sentiment" in many nations. But it is also certain that there has been a wholesome reaction, and every day more and more people would subscribe to another recent admonition: "serious difficulties await us if we persist in believing ourselves free to become richer and richer while the rest of the world be-

comes poorer and poorer." These are words of Senator Ful-
bright, Chairman of the Committee on Foreign Relations of
the Senate.

But if we put aside political and economic matters which,
urgent as they may seem, are determined in large measure
by more far-reaching circumstances and return to the field
of culture, we shall find no less significant symptoms. The
first and perhaps most important of all is the fact that, despite the vicissitudes we have been enumerating, the technical understanding and study of the Ibero-American cultures have increased progressively since the first decades of
the century.

Let us examine a few facts. At the outset it is significant
that the foreign language most studied in the United States
as a whole, if one encompasses the elementary grades and
the four high school years, is Spanish. At Columbia University there are more than thirty persons engaged in teaching
Spanish at various levels, from the practical rudiments of
the language to advanced linguistic, literary, and historical
research. And it is a rare year when two or three doctoral
dissertations and some half-dozen master's essays are not
approved, studies dealing with subjects of Hispanic-American
literature, language, and culture (this does not include those
treating Spanish themes), some of which turn out to be
definitive, and at times unique, contributions to the problems under investigation. This includes only the Hispanic
department and leaves out of consideration the various specialists—geographers, anthropologists, economists, sociolo-
gists, historians, jurists or internationalists, and scientists—
who have either an ancillary interest in Hispanic-American
materials or are exclusively dedicated to their study in their
professional lives.

I am not sure sufficient publicity has been given to the
fact that Columbia University, on the occasion of celebrat-

ing its bicentennial in 1952, a year to be sure in which political relations still left much to be desired, also dedicated
one of the six international conferences it had arranged with
the collaboration of scholars from many countries to the
subject "Responsible Freedom in the Americas." This was
the only conference devoted to the study of a geographical-
cultural area. In meetings held during a six-day period the
problems related to education at its various levels were
studied, as were those related to government, religion, communication of ideas, and the arts. In addition to North
American specialists, a group of Latin-American personalities
was invited, whose names, I believe, were a guarantee of
independence and lack of bias. These included Ricardo J.
Alfaro, Alceu Amoroso Lima, Jorge Basadre, Dantès Belle-
garde (from Haiti), Jaime Benítez, Daniel Cosío Villegas,
Carlos Dávila, Fernando Diez de Medina, Gilberto Freyre,
Jorge García Granados, Max Henríquez Ureña, Bernardo A.
Houssay, Eduardo Jiménez de Aréchaga, Alberto Lleras
Camargo (the guiding figure in the organization of the
conference), Jorge Mañach, Gabriela Mistral, Justo Pastor
Benítez, Mariano Picón-Salas, Galo Plaza, Salvador Salazar
Arrué, Eduardo Santos, Arturo Torres Rioseco, Otilio Ulate,
Rafael Heliodoro Valle, and Silvio Zavala. The papers that
were presented and a résumé of the discussions appeared in
a volume entitled *Responsible Freedom in the Americas*,[21]
but, regrettably, plans for a Spanish edition were unsuccess-
ful.

If I speak of Columbia University it is simply because I
know it best, not because its situation in these matters is
either unique or exceptional. In many other institutions
throughout the country there are Hispanic departments of
equal importance, distinguished professorships, institutes of
Latin-American history, and specialists studying hemispheric
problems.

The bibliography of Hispanic-American topics is extremely rich, including not only literary and linguistic subjects but books and studies on the history, economics, life, education, or natural history of all the countries. In addition to annual repertories such as the *Handbook of Latin American Studies,* published by the University of Florida in collaboration with the Hispanic Foundation of the Library of Congress, and the *Hispanic American Report,* published by Stanford University, numerous learned and technical journals are devoted entirely or in part to Hispanic-American subjects. Two of these, the *Revista Hispánica Moderna* and the *Hispanic American Historical Review,* publish quarterly bibliographies notably complete in their respective fields: literature and history. Holders of fellowships and other types of cultural exchanges are increasing constantly and reaching sizeable proportions.

The foregoing is little more than a very rapid review of certain obvious facts and by no means aspires to be a systematic exposition of the whole field of inter-American studies. It should suffice, nevertheless, to convince my readers that the United States knows the Hispanic-American world much more thoroughly than is generally assumed.

This fact does not invalidate the assertions made at the outset about the ignorance of the average man, or the lack of prestige enjoyed by Hispanic culture in the various strata of the culturally elite, or among the "select minorities," still attentive, as is also the case in the Hispanic-American countries, to the latest literary, philosophical, and artistic fashion of Paris or London.

That both of the foregoing situations exist only demonstrates the superficiality of certain generalizations. The various facts to which we have referred before are independent of political vicissitudes and enjoy an insured continuity; they constitute the solid basis for future understanding.

There are also clear indications that changes in the political atmosphere are going to produce effects, some of them immediate, in the cultural sphere. Many foundations are intensifying their support of programs and projects for Hispanic-American studies, and, within even the three or four coming months, various meetings of an inter-American cultural nature have already been announced. The daily press, almost entirely oblivious of continental matters—save for well-known exceptions such as the New York *Times* and a few other papers—is beginning to realize the existence and importance of the other Americans.[22]

Considered from another point of view, it would be necessary to mention the feeling of insecurity that is again beginning to pervade the American soul. It is important to consider this fact because, were we to analyze history, we would see that the moments of insecurity that Americans have undergone have coincided with the instinctive renewal of continental solidarity. Although Americans may give others the impression of absolute self-confidence and even of offensive conceit, it can be said that few peoples have expressed in their literatures a greater capacity for self-criticism or what we might call anxiety of conscience.

Not long ago uneasiness and disquiet took external and public form as a result of alarm over the "Sputnik." But I am not referring to that so much as to something deeper: to the recent question formulated by Norman Thomas, "Are We as Right as We Think?," or to the statement of a well-known historian when he said, "We are a people in search of ourselves. Constantly, since the birth of our nation, we have tried to discover a mirror in which to see our true image. And this painful uncertainty as to what kind of people we are still distinguishes us among the nations of the world."

Jacques Maritain has spoken of the excessive modesty of

the North American, of his desire to be loved—in the English of the United States one would say "to be accepted"—of his feeling a lack of roots, while, as he comments, "The worst scoundrel in Europe has roots." And it is somewhat paradoxical that while a European like Maritain speaks of the promise of the United States, there has been creeping into the upper intellectual strata for some time—since the McCarthy commotion—a new debate between conformists and nonconformists over whether the promise and the values on which the latter rests are real.

This is doubtless a return, with certain inevitable differences, to an attitude similar to that of the first decades of the century, when Henry Adams denounced the corruption of the American ideal and Henry James brought to his novel the experience of the uprooted Yankee going to Europe in search of a new dream or simply fleeing from his own emptiness. Hence arose the state of mind of the so-called lost generation; the intent to create a new humanism headed by Irving Babbitt and Paul Elmer More; the social criticism of Theodore Dreiser, of Sinclair Lewis, and, a little later, of Dos Passos, Fitzgerald, and Hemingway; or the terribly human depth of O'Neill's dramatic productions and Faulkner's narrative works, both so obsessed by a feeling of guilt.[23]

From that moment of uneasiness, self-criticism, and insecurity came the voice of Waldo Frank who, looking for the roots of his own culture (after writing his *Rediscovery of America*), went first to Europe and then to Hispanic America in search of the spirit he failed to find in his own world. No one in the United States has ever spoken with greater understanding and knowledge, with a greater feeling of continental brotherhood about the complementary character of the two American cultures.

Today no voice like Frank's is heard nor is it likely to be.

The present crisis is of a different sort, but I believe a new period of rapprochement and mutual respect is drawing near.

In conclusion let us ask what is happening in Hispanic America in relation to our problem. We have seen in the case of the United States, on the one hand, the existence of a genuine and rather widespread interest in Hispanic-American studies; on the other, a state of uneasiness coinciding precisely with the moment of its greatest power. Corresponding to the first of these factors, we have in Hispanic America today a much more profound and extensive knowledge of what the United States is than has existed in any other period. Thousands of Hispanic-American students have studied in universities in the United States; many of the leaders of the new democracies have spent their exiles in New York or other cities and, it is only fair to admit, have found refuge and even encouragement—if not in Washington, at least in the ranks of liberal opinion. Even businessmen, north and south, seem to understand one another better, although not always to the benefit of the people. But the present-day Hispanic-American intellectual—and the list of names would be a long one—possesses greater information about and is more aware of what American culture means than those of previous generations: not only concerning its values but also concerning its failures and dangers; not only what can and should be expected from it but also what should be avoided and opposed.

As for the American state of mind, one could adduce a suggestive paradox. The most powerful country in the world and, to some degree, the most aggressive, shows evident signs of disquietude, while in the Latin-American countries, harassed today by the gravest and most urgent problems of all kinds—economic, political, social, and spiritual—I seem to sense the awakening of a feeling of security and confidence, as though among errors and extremes of all sorts they were beginning to steer a course by the compass of their true destiny.

Today the greater part of the Hispanic-American world, as has been the case with other peoples lagging in their march toward modernity, is passing through the tripartite revolution of our time: the technological, the nationalistic, and the social, dedicated to a more equitable distribution of the world's goods and to the struggle for well-being. Recently this situation was cogently defined by Arturo Uslar Pietri at the dedication of a statue to Simón Bolívar in Washington, D.C.:

> Perhaps nowhere in the world at present is there a more dramatic and more vigorous undertaking than that of the twenty Latin-American states to guarantee, not only their political liberty, but freedom from the great social and economic inequalities inherited from the past. That process may lead at times to bloody conflicts and to anarchic explosions. These would be sorely misinterpreted were they viewed as manifestations of a kind of incapacity to live in an orderly fashion; they are, on the contrary, the manifestations of a social organism in search of a kind of justice not to be imposed by the whim of force; in search of a stability that cannot rest on the perpetuation of misery.[24]

And President Figueres has spoken of the three great Hispanic-American milestones: conquest, independence, and today's struggle for social well-being.

Neither through history, nor geography, nor because of the complexity of continental relations can the United States feel itself alien to that struggle. Sooner or later they will have to recognize their responsibility. This they have recognized, as we have seen, in various periods, and I believe they are beginning to recognize it again now. But the peoples of Hispanic America would be making a mistake to expect everything from their aid or even to expect too much;

the governing classes have to recognize their own responsibility and not be swayed by resentments, doubtless well-founded in many cases. Already there are responsible voices that speak of sacrifices and the need of putting their own house in order. It should not be forgotten, either, that the acceptance of all foreign aid implies a certain submission. At the same time the benefactor cannot be expected to relinquish the right to demand certain returns.

It is obvious that we are living in grave times and that there is not much basis for optimism; neither should we surrender to despair. The problems of the two Americas, of the two cultures whose confrontation we have been studying, are linked to the larger crisis through which the contending forces are passing today. If one thinks in historical terms it would not be unreasonable to conceive that from the present struggles there might emerge a period of relative stability, analogous, but in an incomparably broader sphere, to that resulting from the religious struggles of the sixteenth and seventeenth centuries. From that period emerged a rationalistic and liberal Europe; from this, if it comes, can be expected a more humane way of life in which the inequalities and inequities of the past may be tempered and reduced.

As we said at the outset, Toynbee envisages the present dissentions as leading to universal unity; Maritain hopefully contemplates the possibility of a new integral humanism founded on American values; and for many years my friend Juan Larrea, poet and visionary, has been prophesying the reign of the spirit and of poetry, with its center in the lands of America, toward which in his opinion all the signs of history point.

If that golden age arrives, and the alternative according to Toynbee can well be the autogenocide of humanity, each great historical culture will contribute its most genuine values. What, then, should be the guiding principles and the attitude of Hispanic, Iberian, Latin, and Indo-Hispanic America, through whose voice a great tradition is going to speak in the future?

As far as I, an objective observer for many years, am concerned, there is no doubt: on the one hand, it should affirm—overcoming nationalistic aspirations and divisions— the feeling of unity that since Bolívar all of its great men have been proclaiming and desiring. It should heed the lessons of history and of its true nature. But on the other hand, equal to equal, without either surrender or hostility, and preserving, of course, its own character, it should recognize the bonds that unite it with the other parts of the hemisphere: the common destiny of what from the beginning the European saw as a New World; one where, even in these tumultuous times, one can already discern the disappearance of the rivalries of the Old World and the effective synthesis of various cultures.

NOTES

Notes to Part I

1 His remarks may be consulted in the work of José de Onís, *The United States as Seen by Spanish American Writers, 1776–1890* (New York: The Hispanic Institute in the United States, 1952), 12. The reader is referred also to Onís' accurate observations on the conflict between the two cultures and races and the accompanying bibliography on this subject.

2 Charles A. and Mary R. Beard, *The Rise of American Civilization*, (2 vols. in one; New York: Macmillan, 1944), I, 394.

3 Henry Adams, *History of the United States of America* (New York: Antiquarian Press, 1962), 339–40.

4 Samuel Eliot Morison and Henry Steele Commager, *The Growth of the American Republic* (2 vols.; New York: Oxford University Press, 1942), II, 334–35.

5 George Santayana, *The Hermit of Carmel and Other Poems* (New York: Charles Scribner's Sons, 1901), 217, 229.

6 French Ensor Chadwick, *The Relations of the United States and Spain: Diplomacy* (New York: Charles Scribner's Sons, 1909), 93, 587. A work especially recommended for its documentation and objectivity, it is the most complete record of historical relations between the two countries. In the United States there is an enormous bibliography on the different aspects of this subject, from the Louisiana matters and the Florida treaty to the Cuban war. Although less numerous, there are also many studies by Spaniards and Hispanic Americans. We do not deem it within the purview of a general investigation such as the present, however, to engage in an extensive bibliographical exposition.

   As examples of recent résumés of certain sides of the question from the Spanish point of view, the reader is referred to the pam-

phlets by F. Morales Padrón, *Spanish Help in American Independence* (Madrid: Publicaciones Españolas, 1952), 46pp., and Oc-
tavio Gil Munilla, *Spain's Share in the History of the United States
of America* (Madrid: Publicaciones Españolas, 1952), 45pp. Both
form a part of the series "Spanish Topics for the World." Actually
they supply very little new material, but they do afford a synthesis
of their respective subjects.

In the matter of the Cuban war, the final phase of the conflict,
scarcely any reputable American historian has failed to concede
that its basic causes, as well as the stupid acts of Spain (which
finally, although late, was of a mind to yield) were traceable to
the weakness of McKinley, journalistic demagoguery fanned by
Pulitzer and Hearst, and popular hysteria. As a matter of fact, not
long ago a distinguished historian, William E. Leutchenburg, wrote
an interesting article for the review *American Heritage* (VIII
[February, 1957], No. 2), 32–45, entitled "The Needless War With
Spain," under the following epigraph: "The current was too strong,
the demagogues too numerous, the fall elections too near."

7 Stanley T. Williams, *The Spanish Background of American Literature* (2 vols.; New Haven: Yale University Press, 1955), I, xx, 5–
6. Before the work of Williams, the most complete study of the
subject was that of M. Romera Navarro, *El hispanismo en Norteamérica* (Madrid: Renacimiento, 1917), 451pp.

8 Concerning the religious-politico-commercial plans of Sewall and
Mather, consult Harry Bernstein, *Origins of inter-American Interest 1700–1812* (Philadelphia: University of Pennsylvania Press,
1945), 67–69.

9 Harry Bernstein, *Making an inter-American Mind* (Gainesville:
University of Florida Press, 1961), 190pp.

10 Edith Helman, "Early Interest in Spanish in New England (1815–
1835)," *Hispania*, XXIV (1946), 339–51.

11 James F. Shearer, "French and Spanish Works Printed in Charleston, South Carolina," *Papers of the Bibliographical Society of
America*, XXXIV (1940), 137–70.

12 Bernstein, *Origins of inter-American Interest*, 62, 65, *passim*. Other
studies by Bernstein that could be consulted would include "Las
primeras relaciones intelectuales entre New England y el mundo
hispánico, 1700–1815," *Revista Hispánica Moderna*, V (1939) 1–
17; and "Some inter-American Aspects of the Enlightenment,"
Latin America and the Enlightenment, ed. A. P. Whitaker (New
York: Appleton, 1942), 53–69.

13 F. S. Stimson, "Spanish Themes in Early American Literature in
Novels, Drama, and Verse, 1770–1830" (Ph.D. dissertation, University of Michigan), cited in Williams, *Spanish Background*, I, 65.

14 Helman, "Early Interest in Spanish in New England," 343.
15 See Onís, *United States*, for additional information and bibliography; also Charles C. Griffin, *The United States and the Disruption of the Spanish Empire, 1810–1822* (New York: Columbia University Press, 1937), 317pp. Onis has also devoted some study to Foronda. On Letamendi, see James F. Shearer, "Agustín de Letamendi: A Spanish Expatriate in Charleston, S.C. (1825–1829)," *South Carolina Historical and Genealogical Magazine,* XLIII, (1942), 18–26.
16 Williams, *Spanish Background*, I, p. xxvi.
17 Gertrude Stein, *Picasso* (Boston: Beacon Press, 1960), 17–19.
18 Richard Henry Dana, *Two Years Before the Mast,* cited in Williams, *Spanish Background,* I, 89.
19 Iris Lilian Whitman, *Longfellow and Spain* (New York: Instituto de las Españas, 1927), 9, 35.
20 Havelock Ellis, *The Soul of Spain* (New York: Houghton Mifflin, 1915), vii.
21 The bibliography in this area of our subject is voluminous. In the United States, from the period of Moses and Bancroft, there has been an important school of historians of the West and Southwest and of relations with the Spanish world, the most important organ of which is the *Hispanic American Historical Review*. In Spain, in addition to the work of certain historians of the nineteenth century, recent years have seen the appearance of a few outstanding monographic studies. As regards the teaching of Spanish and scholarly research, in addition to various professional reviews, principally the *Hispanic Review* (erudite and critical in character) and *Hispania* (more professional in nature), one can consult Madaline Wallis Nichols, "The History of Spanish and Portuguese Teaching in the United States," in *A Handbook on the Teaching of Spanish and Portuguese,* ed. Henry Grattan Doyle (Boston: D. C. Heath and Co., 1945), 395pp.; and *Handbook of Hispanic Source Materials and Research Organizations in the United States,* ed. Ronald Hilton (Toronto: The University Press, 1942), 441pp.
22 Onís, *United States as Seen,* the first two chapters, especially pages 12–13 and 27–51. Onís deals particularly with the Hispanic Americans; moreover, until the year 1822, which marks the end of chap. 2, there is no clear division between Spaniards and Hispanic Americans.
23 The *Apuntes* of Foronda have been published by José de Onís. See "Valentín de Foronda's Memoir on the United States of North America, 1804," *The Americas,* IV (1948), 351–87.
24 See the English version of Onís' report: *Memoir Upon the Negotiations Between Spain and the United States,* trans. with notes by

Tobias Watkins (Baltimore: E. de Krafft, 1921), 152 pp. For information on Onís consult C. Pereyra, "Un americanista genial (Don Luis de Onís)," *Unión Hispano-Americana,* III (1919), pp. 2–3; Griffin, *United States and the Disruption,* 82–83; and P. C. Brooks, *Diplomacy and the Borderlands: The Adams-Onís Treaty of 1819* (Berkeley: University of California Press, 1939), 262pp.

25 Joseph Blanco White, *The Life of the Rev. Joseph Blanco White Written by Himself; with Portions of his Correspondence;* ed. John Hamilton Thom, (3 vols.; London: Chapman, 1845), III, 295–96.

26 We understand that José de Onís, who kindly showed us a copy, is preparing an edition.

27 Ramón de la Sagra, *Cinq Mois aux Etats-Unis de l'Amérique du Nord, depuis le 29 avril jusqu'au 23 septembre, 1835. Journal de Voyage de M. Ramón de la Sagra, Directeur du Jardin des Plantes de la Havane, et membre de plusieurs Sociétés savantes nationales et étrangères,* traduit de l'Espagnol par M. René Baissas (Bruxelles, Société Typographique Belge, 1837).

28 Mario Méndez Bejarano, *Tassara, nueva biografía crítica* (Madrid: Imprenta de J. Perez, 1928), 94.

29 More than twenty years ago we visited the Spanish Embassy in Washington in search of information on those Spanish writers who had served there. All we could find were a few unorganized, dust-covered files, some of them illegible from dampness, scattered on the floor of a basement room. It was obvious that not a single person, of the many who had passed through there since the nineteenth century, had felt the slightest curiosity about the subject. Faced with such disorder, and having very little time, we had to abandon our attempt.

30 Méndez Bejarano, *Tassara,* 94–95.

31 Cyrus C. De Coster, "Valera en Washington," *Arbor,* XXVIII (1954), 215–23, the most complete résumé; J. L. Cano assembles some brief facts on Valera and the American poets in his article "Juan Ramón Jiménez y la poesía norteamericana," *Revista Shell,* Year 7, (September, 1958), No. 28, pp. 35–38; and Carmen Bravo devotes a chapter to Valera's stay in the United States in her recent *Biografía de Don Juan Valera* (Barcelona: Gredos, 1959), 251–264. De Coster has also included a number of letters written from Washington in the book *Correspondencia de don Juan Valera (1859–1905)* (Valencia: Editorial Castalia, 1956), 82–132. A few others had been published before by Domínguez Bordona in *Revista de Archivos, Bibliotecas y Museos,* II (1925), 237–52, and in *Epistolario de Valera y Menéndez Pelayo* (Madrid: Compañía Iberoamericana de Publicaciones, 1930), 253pp.

32 De Coster, *Correspondencia,* 82.

33 *Ibid.*, 89.
34 *Ibid.*, 134.
35 Juan Valera, *A vuela pluma* (Madrid: Fé, 1897), 133.
36 *Ibid.*, 146–47.
37 *Ibid.*, 163.
38 *Ibid.*, 171–73.
39 *Ibid.*, 303–306, 312.
40 Ronald Hilton, *Campoamor, Spain, and the World* (Toronto: The University Press, 1940), 112–13.
41 John De Lancey Ferguson, *American Literature in Spain* (New York: Columbia University Press, 1916), 267pp.
42 Ferguson lists fifty-eight translations of Cooper to the year 1915; José Fernández Montesinos mentions twenty-one between 1831 and 1847 in his *Introducción a una historia de la novela en España* (Valencia: Editorial Castalia, 1955), 345pp.
43 In the foregoing remarks we have attempted only to emphasize certain facts taken from Ferguson's well-documented book, the source of the foregoing quotations.
44 Ferguson, *American Literature*, 3–4.
45 Harold W. Bentley, *A Dictionary of Spanish Terms in English With Special Reference to the American Southwest* (New York: Columbia University Press, 1932), 243pp.
46 Although they treat the subject in a much more rigorously historical form and quite differently than we, the following studies and their accompanying bibliographies could be consulted profitably: Silvio Zavala, *The Frontiers of Hispanic America*, reprinted from *The Frontier in Perspective*, ed. by Walker D. Wyman and Clifton B. Kroeber (Madison: The University of Wisconsin Press, 1957), 35–58; various articles in *El norte de México y el sur de Estados Unidos* (México: Sociedad Mexicana de Antropología, 1943.
47 *The Autobiography of Alice B. Toklas* (New York: Harcourt, Brace and Co., 1933), 111.
48 Américo Castro, *The Meaning of Spanish Civilization* (Princeton, N.J.: Princeton University Press, 1940), 28–29.

Notes to Part II
1 See Alfonso Reyes, *Ultima Tule* (México: Imprenta Universitaria, 1942), 127.
2 In his book *Viejas polémicas sobre el Nuevo Mundo* (*Comentarios a una tesis de Hegel*) (Lima: Banco de Crédito del Perú, 1944), Gerbi gives a good résumé of the subject and assembles numerous opinions. Although the approach is different, one might also consult Salvador de Madariaga, *The Fall of the Spanish American Empire* (New York: Macmillan, 1948), 443pp.

3 We are following, substantially, the résumé of the discussion made by Ruggero Orfei in his article "Gli Stati Uniti offrono un nuovo tipo di civiltà?" in the review *Vita e Pensiero*, XLII (1959), 20–27.
4 José Ortega y Gasset, "Sobre los Estados Unidos," *Obras completas* (9 vols.; Madrid: Revista de Occidente, 1957–62), IV, 378.
5 Reyes, "Notas sobre la inteligencia americana," *Ultima Tule*, 132.
6 See Américo Castro, *The Structure of Spanish History*, trans. Edmund L. King (Princeton, N.J.: Princeton University Press, 1954), Chap. 2, p. 37 *passim*.
7 See the article of Luis Araquistain in *La Torre*, III (1955), 159–69.
8 Eduardo Caballero Calderón, *Americanos y europeos* (Madrid: Guadarrama, 1957), 248–49.
9 Leopoldo Zea, *América en la historia* (México: Fondo de Cultura Económica, 1957), 17.
10 Leopoldo Zea, "Dos Américas," *Ensayos sobre filosofía en la historia* (México: Stylo, 1948), 181.
11 Angélica Mendoza, *Fuentes del pensamiento de los Estados Unidos*, cited in Zea, *América*, 215.
12 *Ibid.*, 169.
13 Samuel Flagg Bemis, *The Latin American Policy of the United States* (New York: Harcourt, Brace and Co., 1943), 391.
14 Waldo Frank, *America Hispana: a Portrait and a Prospect* (New York: Charles Scribner's Sons, 1931), 274.
15 Zea, *América*, 175, 177.
16 Bemis, *Latin American Policy*, 314–15.
17 Roberto F. Giusti, *Ensayos* (Buenos Aires: Arte Gráfica Bartolomé U. Chiesino, 1955), 226–27.
18 Germán Arciniegas, *El estudiante de la mesa redonda* (Buenos Aires-Barcelona: Editora y Distribuidora Hispano Americana, 1957), 201.
19 Luis Alberto Sánchez, "Un país sin literatura," *Un sudamericano en Norteamérica* (Santiago de Chile: Ercilla, 1942), chap. 5.
20 As has been indicated in the introduction, since the time when these lines were written, the concern and attention of the United States regarding the problems of Hispanic America has increased measurably. Various matters could be adduced in substantiation, but we shall limit ourselves to two or three among the most recent: the establishment of a special commission by President Eisenhower for the study of existing differences with Hispanic America, and the planning of a long-range policy; the conclusions of the American Assembly of Arden House (Columbia University, 1959, p. 209) where, during the month of October there was discussed the question of "The United States and Latin America," with representation from various sectors of the country (government, finance, labor,

education, journalism), and in whose report we read, among other things: "We must identify ourselves with the aspirations of the Latin American peoples for social reforms, higher standards of living, and greater educational opportunities. We are in favor of genuine movements of social change which are consonant with representative democracy"; or the recent suggestion of Nelson Rockefeller (November 19) that the economic union of the hemisphere should be effected.

21 *Responsible Freedom in the Americas,* ed. Angel del Río ("Columbia University Bicentennial Conference Series" [New York: Doubleday, 1955]), 554pp.

22 Paralleling the interest of political or private institutions, scarcely a day passes since these studies were composed that articles do not appear in American newspapers and magazines about the need for a greater understanding of Hispanic-American aspirations and a correction of past errors. We recall, among others, articles by Walter Lippmann, Adolf Berle, and Chester Bowles. All of these are oriented in the direction we have indicated, and reflect the the same spirit that Senator Hubert Humphrey defined some months ago in "A New Era for Latin America," published in *Combate,* San José de Costa Rica (March–April, 1959), 43–51.

23 Although in a somewhat different sense from that in which we are considering it here, Concha Zardoya is perfectly aware of the phenomenon: the uneasiness and nonconformity of a large part of American literature. And thus she writes in the preliminary note to her *Historia,* viii: "A part of the power possessed by American literature stems from the violent opposition of the writer to the political and economic way of life of the country. The best authors and works constitute a living body of protest."

24 *Speech of Doctor Arturo Uslar Pietri, Ambassador Extraordinary of Venezuela, on Special Mission, for the Ceremony of the Inauguration of the Statue of the Liberator, Simón Bolívar, in the City of Washington, February 27, 1959* (Caracas: Tipografía Vargas, S. A., 1959), 6.

DATE DUE

DE 30 '66		
AUG 2 8 '79		
AUG 14 '79		